Textile

EDITED BY
CATHERINE HARPER
AND DORAN ROSS

THE JOURNAL OF
CLOTH AND CULTURE

VOLUME 4
ISSUE 2
SUMMER 2006

ORDERING INFORMATION
Three Issues per volume. One volume per annum. 2006:
Volume 4

ONLINE
www.bergpublishers.com

BY MAIL
Berg Publishers
C/O Turpin Distribution Services
Pegasus Drive
Stratton Business Park
Biggleswade
Bedfordshire SG18 8TQ
UK

BY FAX
+ 44 (0)1767 601640

BY TELEPHONE
+ 44 (0)1767 604951

For Subscription Enquiries
email custserv@turpin-distribution.com

ENQUIRIES
Editorial: Kathryn Earle, Managing Editor,
email kearle@bergpublishers.com

Production: Ken Bruce,
email kbruce@bergpbublishers.com

Advertising: Veruschka Selbach,
email vselbach@bergpublishers.com

SUBSCRIPTION DETAILS
Free Online Subscription for Print Subscribers.

Full color images available online.

Access your electronic subscription through
www.ingentaconnect.com

Institutional base list subscription price:
US$225.00, £125.00

Individuals' subscription price: US$79.00, £46.00

Berg Publishers is the imprint of
Oxford International Publishers Ltd.

AIMS AND SCOPE

Cloth accesses an astonishingly broad range of human experiences. The raw material from which things are made, it has various associations: sensual, somatic, decorative, functional and ritual. Yet although textiles are part of our everyday lives, their very familiarity and accessibility belie a complex set of histories, and invite a range of speculations about their personal, social and cultural meanings. This ability to move within and reference multiple sites gives textiles their potency.

This journal brings together research in textiles in an innovative and distinctive academic forum for all those who share a multifaceted view of textiles within an expanded feld. Representing a dynamic and wide-ranging set of critical practices, it provides a platform for points of departure between art and craft; gender and identity; cloth, body and architecture; labor and technology; techno-design and practice—all situated within the broader contexts of material and visual culture.

Textile invites submissions informed by technology and visual media, history and cultural theory; anthropology; philosophy; political economy and psychoanalysis. It draws on a range of artistic practices, studio and digital work, manufacture and object production.

SUBMISSIONS

Should you have a topic you would like us to consider, please send an abstract of 300–500 words to one of the editors. Notes for Contributors can be found at the back of the journal and style guidelines are available by emailing kbruce@bergpublishers.com or from the Berg website (www.bergpublishers.com).

ISSN: 1475-9756
www.bergpublishers.com

Contents

EDITORS

Catherine Harper
University College for the
Creative Arts at Epsom
Ashley Road
Epsom KT18 5BE
UK
charper@ucreative.ac.uk

Doran Ross
UCLA
Fowler Museum of Cultural History
308 Charles Young Drive
Los Angeles, CA 90095-1549
USA
dross@arts.ucla.edu

Exotic Quilt Patterns and Pattern Names in the 1920s and 1930s

Abstract

A strong characteristic of American popular culture in the 1920s and 1930s was its fascination with all things "oriental," or generally exotic. It was expressed in a multitude of areas, including furniture, fashion, movies and architecture. It was also evident in quiltmaking, an extremely popular pastime of the era, in the preponderance of patchwork patterns that had an exotic theme or name. Sometimes the designs of these patterns directly reflected their exotic names; most often they did not. The reasons for the popularity of exotic pattern names are varied.

Certainly, pattern designers were capitalizing on the fashion for anything oriental. But, as this paper will propose, ladies' magazine publishers and quilt column writers also were reacting to Americans' ambivalence about Asians—their fear of the "yellow peril" mixed with their admiration for Eastern design. By naming and renaming patterns and, more importantly, by mixing oriental, "colonial," and modern imagery and verbiage, they diluted the negative connotations of the exotic and potentially made it more palatable to the tradition-centered quiltmaking world.

MARIN F. HANSON

Marin F. Hanson is Curator of Exhibitions at the International Quilt Study Center at the University of Nebraska-Lincoln, an academic center and museum that encourages the interdisciplinary study of all aspects of quiltmaking and fosters preservation of the tradition. She received her MA in Textile History and Museum Studies from the University of Nebraska-Lincoln and focused her graduate research on the influence of Asian art and culture on American quiltmaking. Her most recent publication was a co-authored paper entitled "Quilts as Manifestations of Cross-Cultural Contact: East-West and Amish-'English' Examples." In *Uncoverings 2004*, published by the American Quilt Study Group.

Textile, Volume 4, Issue 2, pp. 138–163
Reprints available directly from the Publishers.
Photocopying permitted by licence only.
© 2006 Berg. Printed in the United Kingdom.

Exotic Quilt Patterns and Pattern Names in the 1920s and 1930s

Introduction

In the 1920s and 1930s, one of the dominant influences on decorative arts, and on American popular culture in general, was the fascination with anything exotic or oriental. (As a note of clarification, this paper uses the word "oriental" in the way people in the early twentieth century would have used it—as a generic description of a geographic region including North Africa and the Middle East, and extending to countries of the Far East, *and* as a synonym for exotic.) From gardens to home furnishings to Hollywood movies, an oriental atmosphere was fashionable. The exotic style was even popular in the world of quiltmaking, a somewhat surprising fact as quilts often have been associated with a conservative, traditional American esthetic. The exotic quality, however, was frequently granted through the *naming* of a quilt pattern rather than through its design or iconography.

As quilt historian Barbara Brackman (1989: 165–7) has pointed out, quilt pattern names have always been in flux, varying from region to region and changing with national trends and fashions. In the first half of the twentieth century, pattern designers had free rein, not only to "borrow" designs from one another, but also to constantly rename patterns to suit changing fashions. As Brackman puts it:

Competition in the commercial pattern market demands diversity; copyright considerations demand changes in designs originated by others, and marketing demands clever names—all of which have lead [sic] to a long list of patterns and pattern names. (Brackman 1989: 165)

Some of the exotically named patterns that appeared in the 1920–40 heyday of quilt pattern publishing included: Arab Tent, Chinese Gongs, Egyptian Lotus, Formosa Fan, Japanese Garden and Oriental Poppy.

I first discovered the prevalence of 1920s and 1930s exotic patterns and pattern names in conducting research on the influence of Asian art and culture on American quiltmaking. In searching for Asian-inspired quilt blocks in Barbara Brackman's *Encyclopedia of Pieced Quilt Patterns*, the most comprehensive guide to historical quilt patterns, I found a plethora of exotic/oriental pattern names. I then began to search for these exotically named patterns in their original sources as listed in Brackman's *Encyclopedia*: newspaper columns, pattern catalogs, and magazines. While doing so, I discovered that many of the publications in which quilt patterns were common also included images and copy, particularly in advertisements, that referred to the exotic nature of Asia and Asians. It was clear that the prevalence of exotically named quilt patterns was taking place in a larger cultural context of the exoticization of Asian cultures.

A few of the quilt patterns I found actually referenced a motif or image taken from Asian cultures. Others were patterns that could be interpreted as oriental, but which also had been assigned many other, non-exotic names. A large segment of them, however, had little or no connection between their exotic names and the designs they featured. The reason may simply have been that designers, pressured to constantly and quickly produce exciting patterns, gave mainstream quilt blocks (the basic design unit of a patchwork quilt) exotic names in order to follow the trends of the day without having to create something new. I propose, however, that the reason also went deeper, culturally, and stemmed from Americans' ambivalent feelings about Asians.

In an age of anti-Asian immigration policies, negative literary and film depictions of Asians (as most clearly seen in the evil Dr Fu Manchu), and Asia's growing international power, especially that of Japan, Americans often viewed Asians in a negative light. At the same time, they appreciated the exotic quality of decorating and dressing in the oriental style. Americans' conflicted feelings about Asians needed to be considered in presenting exotically named patchwork patterns to the public.

Often, in popular magazines and pattern catalogs of the day, exotic styles were juxtaposed or even mixed with the two other most popular styles of the era—colonial and modern. Quilt historian Virginia Gunn (1991: 96), in her article "Quilts for Milady's Boudoir," explicates how the mixing of styles—in her case, colonial and *moderne*—could help produce "cultural change." Gunn argues that women embraced colonial designs in the early twentieth century, not just as a form of nostalgia or a rejection of Victorianism, but also as a way to allow them to adopt new, and sometimes racy, European fashions. Likewise, this paper will argue that quilt pattern designers and publishers mixed exotic styles with colonial and modern styles in order to subtly introduce oriental—and therefore alluring yet dangerous—qualities into the traditional world of quiltmaking.

To argue this point, I will first present an overview of exotically themed quilt patterns from the 1920s and 1930s. I will then discuss the cultural context within which this explosion of exotic patterns occurred—a context in which oriental imagery was used to illustrate everything from short stories in women's magazines to advertisements for gelatin desserts and women's corsets. Next, I will examine the frequent mixing and combining of oriental, colonial and modern styles and motifs in advertisements, catalogs, and quilt patterns. To explain the possible reasons for the mixing of these styles, I will then discuss the late nineteenth and early twentieth-century American views and popular culture stereotypes of Asians, which were largely dichotomized between the exoticized "other" and the vilified enemy of the West.

Exotic Quilt Patterns and Pattern Names in the 1920s and 1930s

Some quilts made during this era directly reflect the influence of Asian art and design. Take, for instance, a quilt in the collections of the International Quilt Study Center (IQSC) at the University of Nebraska-Lincoln, in which an intricately appliquéd dragon floats on a sumptuous black sateen ground (Figure 1; IQSC: 1997.007.0225). The dragon has five claws and is constructed of brilliant yellow sateen, both of which reflect a knowledge, conscious or unconscious, of traditional Chinese sumptuary laws, as only emperors could wear these symbols and colors. And yet the quilt has an irregular, folk-art feel to it, suggesting that it was an original design, perhaps copied from another source such as a commercially produced embroidered robe or painted shawl, or from printed material obtained from a Chinese attraction at one of the World's Fairs.[1] The maker, therefore, clearly was receptive to the trends of the era, likely without having any direct knowledge of Chinese art or culture.

Another example from the IQSC collections is an Art Deco-style quilt depicting plum blossoms, typical motifs in both Chinese and Japanese art (Figure 2; IQSC: 1997.007.0857). The blossoms sway asymmetrically in a stylized, Japanese fashion while the linear border designs resemble Chinese

Figure 1
Dragon quilt, *c.* 1920–1935. Collection
of the International Quilt Study
Center, 1997.007.0225.

fretwork, background patterns seen in many Chinese textiles. A pattern source has yet to be found for this quilt, though it does look professionally designed. These two quilts indicate that some quilt-makers attempted to create quilts that at least somewhat accurately portrayed symbols or motifs of Asian origin. Often, though, the patterns offered to quiltmakers were based on inaccurate or incomplete knowledge of Asian arts and culture.

Stereotyped images of Asians, particularly Chinese, have been standard fare in America at least since the influx of Chinese immigrants during the nineteenth-century construction of the transcontinental railroads.[2] A typical example of representation of Asians in popular culture can be seen in a *Designs Worth Doing* craft catalog, a production of McKim Studios, the commercial outlet for Ruby Short McKim, one of the most popular pattern designers of the era. In the McKim project entitled "Chinee Phone Pad" (Figure 3; *Designs Worth Doing* 1931a), the figure of a young Chinese boy, given the contemporary slang moniker of "Chinee," is appliquéd onto muslin and a wool braid is attached to his head to represent his queue—the long braid non-Manchu males were required to wear during the Manchu dynasty (1644–1911). A

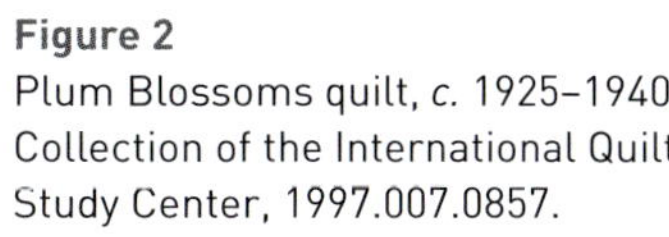

Figure 2
Plum Blossoms quilt, *c.* 1925–1940.
Collection of the International Quilt
Study Center, 1997.007.0857.

pencil is tied to his queue and a paper pad is placed below him. In the illustration of the project, a phone message has been taken in a script that is intended, but fails, to resemble Chinese. While it is true that pre-1911, non-Manchu Chinese men would have worn a queue, by 1928 most Chinese would have cut off their queue, certainly those in the United States (Cook 1931: paras 28–29; Godley 1994: 70). The hairstyle and the pseudo-Chinese script, however, provided a distinctive look with which to immediately identify and differentiate Chinese people, helping to signify them as the exotic "other," rather than a people to whom Americans could truly relate.

The *Kansas City Star*, another popular source for craft and quilt patterns, offered a similar project in the 1930s. Place cards feature a Chinese male figure painted onto cardboard with an embroidery floss queue attached to the back of his head. The author suggests that you "let this Chinese with his braided yarn queue help liven up a chop suey luncheon ..

He is also at your service as an embroidery pattern" ("For Your Oriental Luncheon"). A recipe for "American Chop Suey" is given as well.

Patchwork patterns and kits also featured stereotyped Asian images. A 1928 *Woman's Home Companion* patchwork kit called "Ching and Chow" depicts a Chinese man with a queue accompanied by his dog (Figure 4; *Woman's Home Companion* 1928). A quilt pictured in Thomas Woodard and Blanche Greenstein's *Crib Quilts and Other Small Wonders* features an extremely similar block to the "Ching and Chow" pattern, except that in this version there are

THIS Chinee-boy-pad is easy to make —a braid of yarn is fastened under his applique cap at one end and through ring-top pencil at the other; three very simple-shaped applique patches, some blanket and outline stitches and a glued-on pad complete him.

No. 320 at 20 cents postpaid, includes wax transfers to stamp on muslin, on gay scraps for blouse, trousers and cap, and even on the paper pad. The pad of paper is included as is also the ring-top pencil, wool for his queue, black embroidery floss and instructions so definite that you can't make a mistake.

320 Chinee-phone Pad, all parts .... 20 cents

Figure 3
"Chinee Phone Pad," McKim Studios, 1931.

two human figures facing each other rather than a human and a dog (Figure 5; Woodard and Greenstein 1981: 42). According to the quilt's owner, the quilt was made in the 1930s by her grandmother, probably from a pattern (personal communication, K. Bresenhan, 3 April 2006), a pattern which might have been based, at least in part, on the 1928 *Woman's Home Companion* "Ching and Chow."

Also pictorial, but less stereotyped, were paper lantern patterns. Advertisements of the day show paper lanterns in a variety of settings (Figure 6) and women's magazines provided a multitude of projects using the paper lantern motif.[3] Indeed, a 1931 *Needlecraft—The Magazine of Home Arts* article told women that "Japanese paper lanterns offer numerous suggestions for

THESE amusing patchwork pillows come all cut out ready to sew together. They're jolly and colorful for the sunroom or for a boy's room at home or school. They would also make cunning wall pictures for the nursery or might be used in the center of a quilt of unbleached muslin for a child's bed.

Figure 4
"Ching and Chow," *Woman's Home Companion*, 1928.

Figure 5
Circus Quilt, *c.* 1930–1940. Courtesy:
K. Bresenhan.

decorative novelties … [and] possess a certain charm which assures their popularity at bridge parties or bazaars" (Stevens 1931: 9). The article goes on to give directions for embellishing tablecloths, napkins, and cushions with colorful embroidered and appliquéd lantern motifs.

Several paper lantern quilt patterns appeared throughout the 1930s. They were usually called Chinese Lantern or Japanese Lantern, although in one case the pattern is called Japanese Garden (Figure 7; Brackman 1993: 134–5; Cabot 1933a; *Kansas City Star* 1934). *Aunt Martha*—a quilt pattern catalog, Nancy Cabot—the *Chicago Tribune*'s quilt pattern designer, and the *Kansas City Star* all offered their own lanterns (Brackman 1993: 134–5). Several of these lanterns, however, are exactly or virtually the same pattern, providing evidence that pattern purveyors commonly "borrowed" from one another.

Other patterns with exotic names were less clearly oriental in style, but could, if the designer wished, be interpreted that way. For instance, the McKim Studios catalog offered an Oriental Poppy pattern in 1931 (Figure 8; *Designs Worth Doing* 1931b). Although the poppy motif provided McKim with a direct visual link to the orient, it is clear from its streamlined, modern appearance that names were somewhat arbitrarily assigned. Further evidence for this is the fact that Carrie Hall, in her 1935 book co-authored with Rose Kretsinger, *The Romance of the Patchwork Quilt in America*, named the very same pattern Modernistic California Poppy (Hall and Kretsinger 1935: 106–7).

Along with Dresden Plate, Grandmother's Flower Garden, and Double Wedding Ring, fan variations were the most popular quilt patterns of the era. After

their popularity during the late nineteenth-century crazy quilt fad—a trend for making elaborately embellished and asymmetrically pieced quilts that were largely influenced by Asian art and design —fans reappeared in the 1920s and 1930s. Usually they were either given oriental names such as Formosa Fan (Figure 9; Cabot 1936a), Japanese Fan, and Imperial Fan or old-fashioned ones such as Grandmother's Fan (Brackman 1993: 398–9). A design called Chinese Fan was offered by Nancy Cabot, the pseudonymous 1930s–1940s quilt pattern designer for the *Chicago Tribune* (Figures 10 and 11; Cabot 1943); however, this Chinese Fan pattern greatly resembles Cabot's own Path of Fans and Mohawk Trail patterns (Brackman 1993: 404–5; Cabot 1933b). Pieced somewhat differently but having the same block setting and overall appearance, the three patterns look remarkably alike, again

Figure 6
P. N. Practical Front Corset advertisement, 1925.

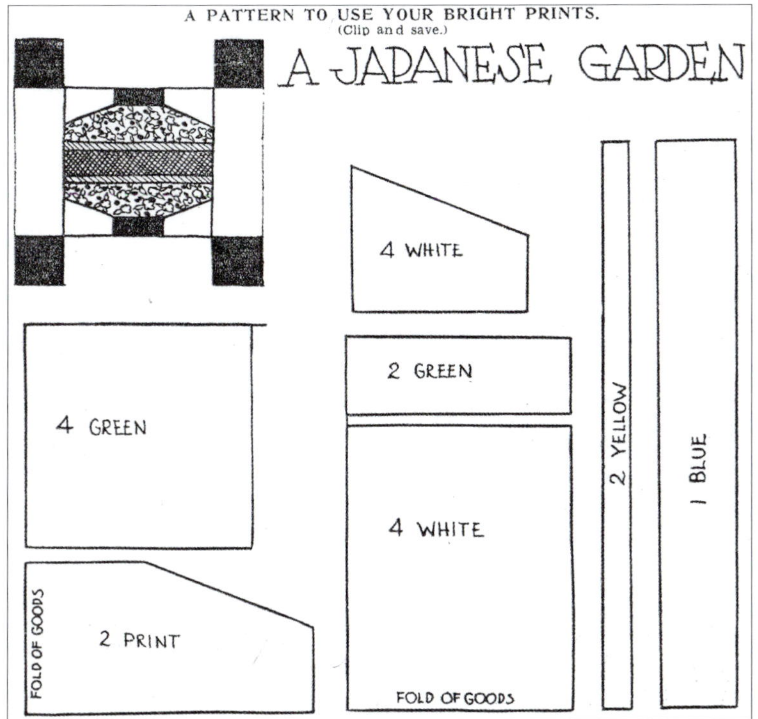

Figure 7
Japanese Garden quilt pattern, 1934.
Courtesy: *Kansas City Star*.

ONE woman said, "Before I catch the quilt fever, I'll have to see a pattern that's entirely different and stunningly beautiful!" The Oriental Poppy is in answer, and beside filling those requirements it is really quite simple to make. The pieced poppy is all straight sewing, the sort that may be run up on the sewing machine, while the bottom half of the block has two leaves and a stem that whips down by hand.

The original was gorgeous in two values of red, a flame and a scarlet, with the flower center of black, boilproof of course, and green applique.

The pattern is No. 380 at 20 cents with material for a sample block to finish about 15 inches square is No. 380X at 40 cents. For an entire quilt top, 5½ blocks long by 5 wide—or about 72x80 inches after all seams are off, you will require 9 1-3 yards. We select this for you in beautiful 80-square cambric finish material as No. 380M at $3.25—pattern included.

We can also supply this with all of the pieces ready cut as No. 380C at $4.50 postpaid.

380 Pattern poppy quilt	$ .20
380X Material for block	.40
380M Material for quilt	3.25
380C Ready cut quilt top	4.50

Figure 8
Oriental Poppy quilt pattern,
McKim Studios, 1931.

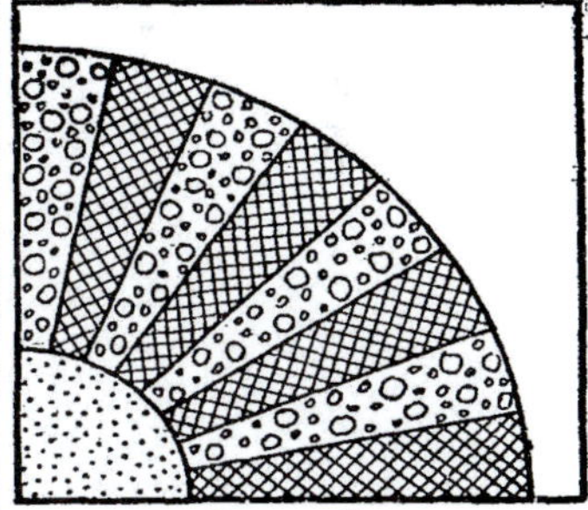

Simple Quilt Has "Formosa Fan" as Attractive Theme

Patterns of this design are 5 cents, stamps or coin. Address Nancy Cabot, Chicago Tribune, or call at one of the Tribune Public Service offices: One South Dearborn street or Tribune Tower.

BY NANCY CABOT.

"Formosa Fan" is another applique quilt pattern of the fan variety, but most attractive and simple to make. The sticks of the fan may be gleaned from the scrap bag, with each a different color, or there may be alternate shades in the fan. Variety may be had by making each applique block different. The interesting quilt diagram accompanying the quilt pattern illustrates a most attractive arrangement of blocks in a quilt composed entirely of applique designs.

Figure 9
Nancy Cabot's Formosa Fan quilt
pattern, 1936.

A quilt created from the "Chinese Fan" pattern is a simple and easy patchwork chore which may be done by any one. Scraps from the rag bag furnish the material for the prints, and the plain color may in any harmonious or contrasting hue. This type of needlework is excellent for idle moments on hot summer days.

pointing to capriciousness in pattern naming.

While some quilt patterns exhibited Asian-inspired motifs or could be interpreted as "oriental," others seemed to be exotic in name only. One designer with an affinity for exotic pattern names was Loretta Leitner Rising, the writer of the *Chicago Tribune*'s Nancy Cabot pattern column. Because the Nancy Cabot column was so widely

Figure 11
Quilt in the Chinese Fan pattern, *c.* 1930–1940. Collection of the International Quilt Study Center, 1997.007.0366.

syndicated (under many different names), with a pattern count eventually numbering over two thousand, her designs would have been seen by women all over the country (Brackman 1991: 22).

In writing about Nancy Cabot's frequent publication of "colonial" patterns, quilt historian Barbara Brackman states, "Interest in colonial antiques during the 1930s dictated that quilt patterns have a historical connection, accurate or not ... therefore the Cabot column is a poor source for quilt history; the newspaper writer tossed in dates and facts with abandon" (Brackman 1991: 23). The same could be said for her presentation of "oriental" patterns; more often than not, her exotically named patterns had little or no connection to their appearance.

She was not alone in doing this, however. Pattern designers from many different publications assigned exotic names to generic patterns. For example, one simple four-pointed star, an elaboration on the common Periwinkle pattern, was named Oriental Star by Nancy Cabot (Figure 12; Cabot 1933c) and Dervish Star by *Grandma Dexter* (Brackman 1993: 474–5). Another set of stars—variously called Chinese Star or Oriental Star by farm newspaper *Rural New Yorker*, pattern catalogs *Grandmother Clark* and *Grandma Dexter*, and author Carrie Hall—is a very close relative of a series of patterns based on a circular crown-like motif. In fact, some of its more popular names are Caesar's Crown, King David's Crown, and Victoria's Crown (Brackman 1993: 436–7).

When the magazine *Home Art's* hexagonal Oriental Splendor blocks are put together in a whole quilt, they create a wonderfully graphic image (Brackman 1993: 52–3). Nancy Cabot, who also published the pattern under the same name, introduced it by stating, "strangely enough, this pattern, which originated in Connecticut in the earliest days of its history, and which was then called 'Many Paths,' is now called 'Oriental Splendor'" (Figure 13; Cabot 1933d). Also strangely enough, a 1935 issue of the magazine *Progressive Farmer* called the pattern Smoothing Iron, again demonstrating that designs were subject to broad interpretation and could be given a wide variety of names, some of them exotic, some of them prosaic (Brackman 1993: 52–3).

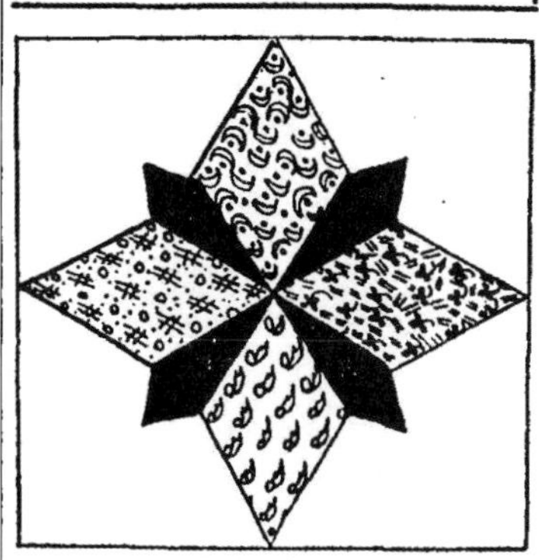

Figure 12
Nancy Cabot's Oriental Star quilt pattern, 1933.

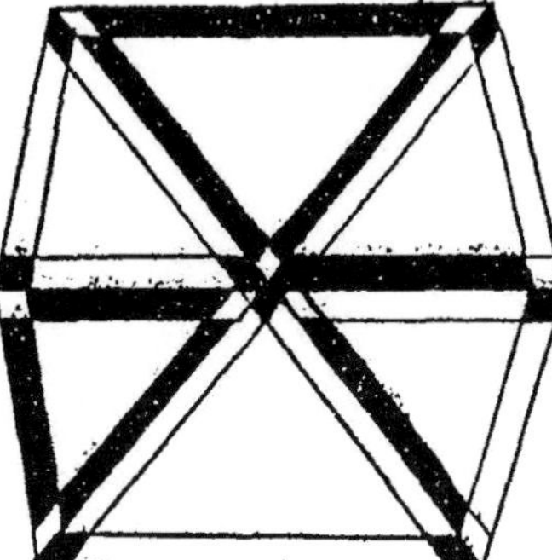

Figure 13
Nancy Cabot's Oriental Splendor quilt pattern, 1933.

Nancy Cabot's inspiration for the naming of Chinese Coin (Figure 14), a pattern with a "hole" (a lighter-colored square) in the center of it, is clearly based on its resemblance to traditional Chinese coins, which had holes in the center and would have been held together on long strings. She fancifully described the pattern's development this way:

An adventurous wanderer returned from the Far East, landed in New York about 1869 and brought with him many souvenirs of his wanderings. He presented to his lady fair,

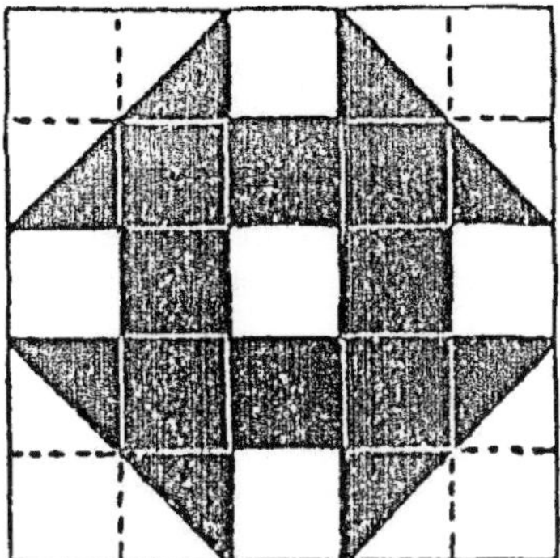

Patterns of this quilt design are 5 cents each, stamps or coin. Address Nancy Cabot, Chicago Tribune, or call at one of the Tribune Public Service offices, One South Dearborn street or Tribune Tower.

Chinese Coin

BY NANCY CABOT.

An adventurous wanderer returned from the far east, landed in New York about 1869, and brought with him many souvenirs of his wanderings. He presented to his lady fair, among other gifts, a rare curio, a Chinese coin. Intrigued with the then unusual token, the enterprising young lady worked the coin into a quilt design. Today we still have the lovely pieced block, "Chinese Coin."

Figure 14
Nancy Cabot's Chinese Coin quilt pattern, 1934.

among other gifts, a rare curio, a Chinese coin. Intrigued with the then unusual token, the enterprising young lady worked the coin into a quilt design. Today we still have the lovely pieced block, Chinese Coin. (Cabot 1934)

By telling this story, Nancy Cabot made the pattern appealing both in its exotic and its "historical" nature. The pattern is a well-known traditional one whose name Double Wrench dates from as early as 1884. It is known most commonly, however, as Hole in the Barn Door, Monkey Wrench, or Churn Dash (Brackman 1993: 234–5). It seems likely that most people would have known this pattern by its other, older names, but re-introducing it with an oriental title gave it an exotic allure.

Chinese 10,000 Perfections is one of many names given to swastika variation patterns (Hall and Kretsinger 1935: 94–5). The swastika is a symbol common to many cultures, and in China it is similar to the character "wan," signifying 10,000. A common expression in China is "wan sui," meaning "may you live 10,000 years." Chinese 10,000 Perfections is therefore an appropriate name for this pattern; however, the pattern was also called Indian Emblem, Flyfoot, Battle Ax of Thor, Mound Builders, and Wind Power of the Osages (Brackman 1993: 158–9). Many cultures are represented in these names and an exotic effect seems to be the common denominator.

Cultural Context for the Abundance of Exotic Pattern Names

Attraction to an oriental mystique in the quilting world did not, of course, occur in a vacuum. Americans, in general, were fascinated with Asian cultures and peoples throughout this period. In the nineteenth century, national magazines had helped the crazy quilt—another oriental-inspired quilt style—become one of the first quilting fads. A few decades later

in the 1910s and 1920s, Paul Poiret became famous for his exotic, and sometimes risqué couture designs. His fashions, inspired by Leon Bakst's costumes for the popular *Ballets Russes* production of *Scheherezade,* were clearly based on oriental imagery. The desire for exotic costume trickled down into the everyday culture of America, resulting in "boudoir" fashions for women that included harem pants, kimonos, and turbans (Gunn 1991).

The broader decorative arts were similarly influenced. Motifs such as Chinese and Japanese-style fans and butterflies were popular, as were new Art Deco designs that displayed a variety of oriental influences. Eighteenth-century Chinese Chippendale-style furniture experienced a revival in the 1920s and 1930s and featured Chinese "fretwork"—linear background designs—that became part of the Art Deco design vocabulary. Even popular architecture reflected the influence of exotic cultures. For example, Chinese and Egyptian-themed movie theatres sprang up all over the country, including the famous Grauman's Chinese Theatre in Hollywood.

Women's magazines were another source of oriental imagery. Early twentieth-century popular magazines often featured representations of Asians, both in literary and artistic format. Pearl S. Buck, author of *The Good Earth*, was responsible for several of these, with short stories such as "The Exile," the tale of a woman who becomes a missionary in China (Figure 15), and "Hearts Come Home," the story of a foreign-educated

Chinese couple who falls in love in Shanghai (Buck 1935a: 15; 1935b: 5). Other stories with exotic themes included those about Westerners living in India or about the desert life of Arab sheikhs (Caher 1931: 13; Bercovici 1931: 8). All of these stories featured lavish illustrations depicting the exotic, and sometimes depraved, lives the Asian characters led.

Advertisements in women's magazines also used oriental imagery and fashions to help sell their products. For instance, an advertisement in the October 1925 *Ladies' Home Journal* pictures a brilliant yellow, white and orange molded Jell-O brand gelatin dessert with a bronze statue of a Chinese mandarin (government official) towering behind it (*Ladies Home Journal* 1925a). Also in 1925, Kodak Cameras ran an advertisement featuring a group of vacationers at the seaside, one relaxing under the shade of a Japanese parasol (*Ladies Home Journal* 1925b). In the same year, Palmolive advertised their soap using the image of a white woman outfitted in harem garb, accompanied by a dark-skinned female servant (*Ladies Home Journal* 1925c).

Department store catalogs offered oriental knick-knacks to add an exotic flair to home interiors. The 1927 Sears, Roebuck catalog, for instance, featured a three-page spread entitled "Gifts

Figure 15
Illustration from Pearl S. Buck's "The Exile," *Woman's Home Companion*, 1935.

from the Orient" and "Decorative Oriental Pottery." In it, one could find dragon-shaped brass dinner gongs, Buddha incense burners, and silk parasol-shaped lamp shades (Mirken 1970: 238–40).

In addition to purchasing ready-made oriental objects, women were encouraged to make their own decorative handwork following patterns with Asian-inspired designs. A set of Japanese lantern table linens in the author's collection was made over 75 years ago by her great-grandmother from a 1927 *McCall Needlework and Decorative Arts* pattern (Figure 16; *McCall Needlework and Decorative Arts* 1927a). The McKim Studios' *Designs Worth Doing* catalogs offered several oriental-inspired projects, including: "Table Mats in Chinese Design" (1930a), "A Beautiful Persian Monogram"

(1930b), and, for the children, "Charming Dollies from Japan" (1931c). The *Kansas City Star* featured embroidery designs called "The Pines of Japan" (1933a) and "The Sacred Mountain in Japanese Motif" (1933b). It is no surprise, then, that so many exotically named quilt patterns also appeared during this era.

The Mixing of Oriental, Colonial and Modern Styles

What *is* surprising is the frequent mixing of oriental styles with colonial and modern styles. At first glance, these styles do not seem to mix readily. The colonial style was a product of the Colonial Revival, a design movement that reflected Americans' growing interest in their colonial and republican past. Originally an architectural movement begun in the last

quarter of the nineteenth century, the Colonial Revival eventually spread to all areas of the decorative arts and interior design, affecting quilts and quiltmaking by the turn of the twentieth century. Reacting to the fussiness of the late-Victorian Aesthetic Movement, colonial styles emphasized clean and spare decorating. Modern styles also stressed cleanliness and functionality. Inspired by the Arts and Crafts, Art Nouveau, and Art Deco movements, modern styles presented streamlined surface decoration and placed a greater emphasis on practicality and usefulness. The esthetic of both colonial and modern styles was very different from the lush, exotic look of oriental styles—which made for interesting results when they were mixed.

Figure 16
Embroidered Japanese lantern table linens. Collection of the author.

The cover of the March 1928 issue of the magazine *Woman's Home Companion* exemplifies these odd juxtapositions. It pictures a miniature tableau of artfully arranged porcelain statuettes. A blue and white Chinese mandarin sits behind two colonial-style figurines, a Little Bo Peep-type female and a chimney-sweep male in a top hat (Figure 17). Admittedly, this unexpected combination most likely portrays the 1845 Hans Christian Andersen tale of the Shepherdess and the Chimney Sweep; however, no indication of this fact is given in the magazine and it does not directly relate to any of the articles inside the issue. Readers probably would not have immediately made the fairy-tale association and on a purely esthetic basis would have viewed the tableau for what it was, a mixture of some of the most common styles of the day. Although the combination may seem anomalous to us today, an examination of 1920s and 1930s needlework sources reveals a pattern of similar style mixtures.[4]

For instance, the 1930–31 edition of McKim Studios' *Designs Worth Doing* catalog advertises a pattern for "Chinese Appliqué Towels" embroidered with "Japanese [not Chinese, as the pattern name stated] lanterns on one and a parasol on the other" (Figure 18; *Designs Worth Doing* 1930c). Pictured putting away the towels into a colonial-style chest is a modern woman, as signified by her short skirt and pumps, depicted in silhouette (a popular way to visually reference colonial-era silhouette profile portraits). In the same issue, McKim presents a pattern for decorating furniture with painted "discs of Chinese type" and "typical pagodas, small figures, willow trees and a bridge" (Figure 19; *Designs Worth Doing* 1930d). The furniture pictured, however, is clearly in the colonial style, with one example being a colonial tilt-top table, the type with a top that tilts to a vertical position for easy storage.

In the world of quilt patterns, the *Chicago Tribune*'s Nancy Cabot often mixed exotic pattern names with descriptions that included colonial or modern references. In some cases, she used references to the original thirteen American colonies to add an air of antiquity. For instance, of Oriental Poppy she says, "The early history of this pattern has Connecticut as its locale" (Cabot 1935); and of Oriental Splendor she says it "originated in Connecticut in the earliest days of its history" (Cabot 1933d). In other cases, she uses words like "birthplace" and "coverlet" to evoke the pride in American history that was at the core of the Colonial Revival. Describing Japanese Poppy, she says, "Ohio is identified as the birthplace of [this] quilt … a coverlet composed of a combination of pieced and plain materials" (Cabot 1936b). Cabot's headlines for the Oriental Tulip (Figures 20 and 21) and Oriental Poppy patterns exhibit her mixing the exotic with modern. For the one she states, "Out of Ancient Egypt Comes Gay Design for 'Modern Quilt" (Cabot 1933e) and for the other, "'Oriental Poppy' is Quilt Showing Modern Harmony" (Cabot 1935).

Creating your own heirloom to pass on to future generations

Figure 17
Cover of *Woman's Home Companion*, March 1928.

Figure 18
"Chinese Appliqué Towels," McKim
Studios, 1930.

was another theme of the Colonial Revival. The 1933 edition of the catalog *Hope Winslow's Quilt Book* advertised a page of patterns under the heading, "A Quilt Created by Your Own Hands Becomes a Greater Treasure as the Years Roll On." Among these patterns are the colonially named Lafayette Orange Peel, the pioneer-themed Rocky Road to California, and the exotic Oriental Splendor (*Hope Winslow's Quilt Book* 1933a). A few pages later, the Chinese Lantern Quilt—"one of the modern patchwork quilt designs that you will enjoy making" (*Hope Winslow's Quilt Book* 1933b)—is on the same page as Dolly Madison Stars and opposite the page entitled "Early American Quilts Are First in Favor Today" (Early American Quilts 1933c).

Another reason why oriental, colonial and modern references were so easily mixed in patchwork-related publications is that many of the exotically named patterns could have fit stylistically into either of the other two genres. Some of them are very basic, geometric quilt blocks that reflect the spare simplicity embodied by the Colonial Revival. For instance, The Chinese Block Quilt, published by the *Kansas City Star* in 1938, is an uncomplicated geometric pattern that would have looked right at home in a colonial-style bedroom, especially if it were completed in a red and white or blue and white color scheme, thereby referencing colonial-era two-color woven coverlets (Figure 22). Indeed, the *Star* admitted that "The Chinese block is a new name for an old pattern," granting the pattern both an exotic and an old-fashioned air (*Kansas City Star* 1938).

Other patterns, such as Oriental Tulip (Figure 20; Cabot 1933e) and Japanese Poppy (Figure 23) by Nancy Cabot (1936b), and Oriental Poppy (*Designs Worth Doing* 1931b) by McKim Studios, revealed a basis in modern design despite their exotic names. Nancy Cabot claims

Figure 19
Chinese decoration on colonial-style furniture, McKim Studios, 1930.

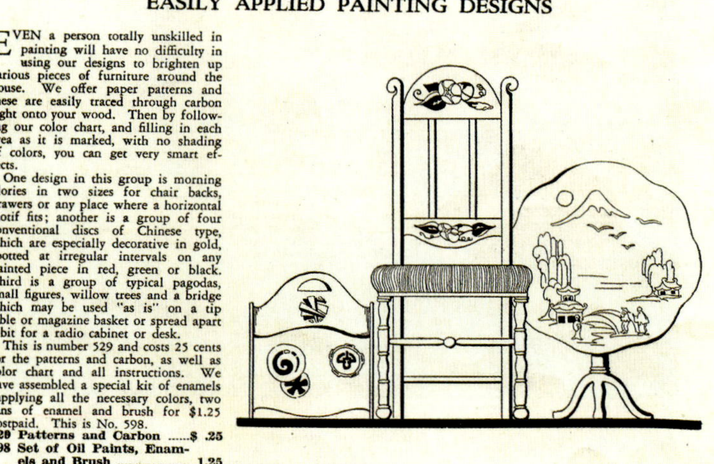

Figure 20
Nancy Cabot's Oriental Poppy quilt pattern, 1935.

Figure 21
Quilt in the Oriental Tulip pattern, *c.* 1930–1940. Collection of the International Quilt Study Center, 2003.003.0141.

Figure 22
The Chinese Block quilt pattern, 1938. Courtesy: *Kansas City Star.*

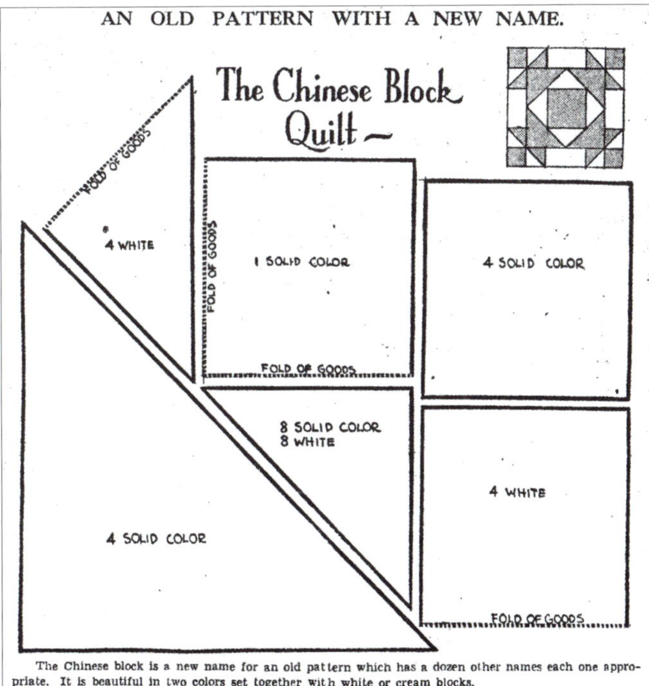

Figure 23
Nancy Cabot's Japanese Poppy quilt
pattern, 1936.

Quilt Pattern Is Popular One in Rural Districts

Patterns of this design are 5 cents, stamps or coin. Address Nancy Cabot, Chicago Tribune, or call at one of the Tribune Public Service offices: One South Dearborn street or Tribune Tower.

Japanese Poppy.

BY NANCY CABOT.

"Japanese Poppy" is one of the floral designs seen on various clothes lines when quilts are put out for their spring airing. One is apt to see more quilts of this pattern in small towns throughout the country than in the city. Ohio is identified as the birthplace of the quilt illustrated today, a coverlet composed of a combination of pieced and plain materials. The blocks are set together in an alternate arrangement, and only 15 applique and 15 plain blocks are used.

catch the quilt fever, I'll have to see a pattern that's entirely different and stunningly beautiful!' The Oriental Poppy is in answer [to her request] ..." (*Designs Worth Doing* 1931b).

If the juxtaposing of oriental styles with colonial and modern styles was so common, what were the reasons? One might be that by referencing the most popular decorating styles of the day, publishers could hedge their bets and sell more patterns. But deeper reasons emerge when we examine how Asians were perceived in late-nineteenth and early-twentieth century America.

American Perceptions of Asians in the Late-Nineteenth and Early Twentieth Century

Ever since Chinese workers first started immigrating in large numbers to the United States in the mid-nineteenth century, first drawn by the gold rush and then by employment in building the transcontinental railroads, Americans have exhibited anti-Asian sentiment. Opposition to Asian immigration was often stated in economic terms, citing the flood of Chinese workers into the American labor force. The Chinese Exclusion Act of 1882— which severely restricted Chinese immigration into the United States—and other anti-Chinese legislation reflected many people's frustration over a perceived loss of jobs due to the influx of Chinese workers (Hing 1993: 22–3).[5] Soon, anti-immigration and anti-naturalization laws spread to cover other Asian nationalities, for instance the 1917 Immigration Act, which included an "Asiatic Barred

in her description of Oriental Tulip that it is a "reproduction of an old Egyptian design that used to be embroidered on robes and temple hangings" (Cabot 1933e). What is more apparent, however, is the pattern's Art Deco sensibility, with its geometric stylization of the tulip form. The McKim Studios' description of Oriental Poppy (Figure 8) ignores its exotic name entirely, emphasizing instead the new and modern aspect of the design: "One woman said, 'Before I

Zone" (Lee 1999: 108). By 1924, almost all Asian nationalities were virtually barred from immigrating to the United States (Hing 1993: 33).

Anti-Asian sentiment was also based in nativist, racist and xenophobic fears. Americans in the late-nineteenth and early twentieth century were engaged in a process of attempting to define what it meant to be American and many people wanted to exclude Asians from this definition, thereby retaining "racial purity" (Hing 1993: 22). For instance, despite the fact that Irish immigrants had been severely discriminated against back East, on the West Coast many of them were the most vocally opposed to Asian immigration (Hing 1993: 21). Historical events also increased Americans' unease about the East, in particular the 1900 Boxer Rebellion, in which hundreds of Westerners were held siege in Beijing by rebels opposed to growing western influence in China. Just five years later, "this anxiety over a 'Yellow Peril' assumed the status of a nightmare after Japan's stunning military victory over Russia" (Lee 1999: 106).

The evil, plotting Dr. Fu Manchu was born out of these fears. Originally a character in a series of novels by the British author Arthur Henry Sarsfield Ward (using the pseudonym Sax Rohmer), Fu Manchu became a frequent movie character as well. His character was that of a sinister genius, head of a worldwide organization dedicated to the downfall of Western institutions and power. Indeed, the "'Asiatic' threat that… [the character of] Fu Manchu represents

is explicitly the threat of racial annihilation" (Lee 1999: 114); he is the personification of the 'Yellow Peril.'"

Providing a counterpoint to Fu Manchu was Charlie Chan, who, though extremely stereotyped, represented the grudging respect Westerners still had for the wisdom supposedly inherent in the Chinese culture. Originally a figure in popular fiction, Charlie Chan (the creation of author Earl Derr Biggers) also became a movie character, ironically first being played by Warner Oland, the Swedish actor who later played Fu Manchu in several movies. The Charlie Chan character was a Chinese-born Honolulu detective who, using his ancient and wise Eastern knowledge, solved cases that his white counterparts were unable to. While still a caricature, speaking in pidgin English and supposedly Chinese aphorisms, he represented a moral contrast to Fu Manchu. He and Fu Manchu came to embody the West's ambivalence about the East, the former a member of an ancient and refined culture, the latter a symbol of the Yellow Peril.

Ironically, during this same period, Asian-inspired fashions and decorating styles went through successive waves of popularity. In 1876, for instance, the US centennial exposition in Philadelphia introduced Americans to Japanese art and design, which fueled the popularity of decorating with Japanese/Chinese (distinctions between these two cultures were often blurred) fans, parasols, porcelain and silks. An obsession with Asian art and design also led to the first quilt

fad, the craze for crazy quilts between 1880 and 1900. Fashions were similarly influenced: articles of clothing such as kimonos and Chinese-style robes and accessories such as parasols and fans became *de rigeur* in the early twentieth century, eventually becoming so embedded that the styles began to be combined with each other and with other, non-Asian styles (Kim and DeLong 1992: 27).

Conclusion

Because of Americans' mixed feelings about the moral character of Asians, women may have been equally unsure of how to view the prevalence of Asian styles and motifs in fashion, advertising, decorating catalogs and even in their quilt patterns. On the one hand, the American public appreciated the exotic quality associated with the Orient, especially when sanitized and safely incorporated into their daily lives, as in architecture, interior decoration or fashion. On the other, the allure of the East was often associated with fears of Asian world domination and also with a sinister and deviant sexuality. Film historian Gina Marchetti points to two common movie characterizations of Asian women to explicate this threatening sexuality. These archetypes, in turn, symbolically represent the entire oriental world:

The "dragon lady" and the "lotus blossom" form two halves of one coin in the popular Western imagination. Seductive and exotic, the former must be forced into submission, while the latter innately recognizes

Western superiority and freely acquiesces to the will of her white master/lover. However, both represent equally taboo desires that must be contained, and their inevitable deaths symbolize the vanquishing of those desires in the name of white "civilization." (Marchetti 2004: 188)

As presented in the movies and various other pop cultural forums, the East was viewed as a place that needed to be conquered, not culturally incorporated.

But, as demonstrated in Gunn's study of "milady's boudoir," the hesitation about adopting new, somewhat suspect fashions could be overcome. Gunn refers to the new early twentieth-century boudoir fashions—which, although inspired by France, included oriental kimonos, turbans, and harem pants—as being perceived originally as "scandalous and languorous" (Gunn 1991: 84). She claims, however, that women, encouraged by ladies' magazines, simultaneously adopted colonial styles in order to soften the indecent nature of the boudoir attire and to bring in the new, *moderne* styles from Europe. She says that, "American women used the colonial revival emphasis, which at first glance looks like a rejection of modern ideas, as a strategy to rationalize the adoption of new French fashion and furnishings" (Gunn 1991: 83). Therefore, by the 1920s and 1930s, these fashions had become fairly widespread, despite their exotic, sexy overtones. Indeed, in 1927, *McCall Needlework and Decorative Arts* presented Chinese-style cropped-pants pajamas and flowing Japanese-style kimonos for American women to purchase and decorate with embroidery or paint (*McCall Needlework and Decorative Arts* 1927b,c). In 1930, Sears and Roebuck offered ready-to-wear "Stylish Japanese Lounging Garments" to American women (Sears and Roebuck 1930: 348). By mixing the three component boudoir styles in their advertising and articles, women's magazines made the exotic and modern components more acceptable to their audience.

If the strategy of using the apparent safety of the "traditional" colonial style to introduce *art moderne* and sexy, oriental-inspired lingerie to American women was successful, why couldn't it be used to introduce exotic quilt patterns to them as well? The quilt designers and pattern publishers were not merely following trends by giving so many of their quilt patterns exotic names. They were also participating in a strategy to make the exotic, with its partly sinister, morally ambiguous, and sexy subtext, more acceptable to the American public. Quiltmaking was perceived as a wholesome activity, an expression of the solid, frugal and morally sound character of early Americans. Pattern designers and publishers could not risk sullying it with too strong an oriental flavor.

Publications therefore used a range of methods to tone down exotic styles and make them more acceptable to American readers. By simply giving traditional, standard quilt blocks oriental names, designers diluted any overtly exotic qualities. By constantly renaming quilt patterns, sometimes with oriental names and sometimes with ordinary ones, they weakened their exotic character. And finally, by juxtaposing and mixing oriental styles with colonial and modern styles in advertising, patchwork designs and quilt descriptions, they made the exotic styles palatable to the American quiltmaking public.

Notes

1. Asian motifs often were used on women's dressing gowns and shawls; for instance, the Spring 1927 *McCall Needlework and Decorative Arts* advertises an exotic peacock outline transfer to be used in painting on an "exquisite evening wrap" (p. 29). World's Fairs also provided images that could have been used as inspiration for quiltmakers; for instance, visitors to the Chinese Lama Temple at Chicago's 1933–4 Century of Progress World's Fair could obtain a pamphlet with an impressive dragon on the cover. For an image, see http://www. ccamuseum.org/Jehol_Temple_ Pamphlet-web.jpg (accessed 30 March, 2006).
2. For various perspectives on how Asians have been viewed throughout American history, see Lee (1999).
3. See, for example, "Design for Rainbow Bridge Set," advertisement in *McCall Needlework and Decorative Arts* (Spring 1927: 46).
4. Although numerous sources were examined for style-mixing content, a more thorough and analytical study of an even wider range of publications

would further add to this research.
5. See http://www. ourdocuments.gov/doc. php?flash=true&doc=47 for the original full text of the Chinese Exclusion Act 1882.

References

Bercovici, Konrad. 1931. "Thirst." *Ladies Home Journal*, January: 8.

Brackman, Barbara. 1989. *Clues in the Calico*. McClean, VA: E.P.M. Publications.

——. 1991. "Who was Nancy Cabot?" *Quilter's Newsletter Magazine*, January/February: 22.

——. 1993. *Encyclopedia of Pieced Quilt Patterns*. Paducah, KY: American Quilter's Society.

Buck, Pearl S. 1935a. "The Exile, Part Two." *Woman's Home Companion*, November: 15.

——. 1935b. "Hearts Come Home." *Ladies Home Journal*, August: 5.

Cabot, Nancy. 1933a. "Interesting Quilt Will Utilize All Small Remnants." *Chicago Tribune*, 20 June: 19.

——. 1933b. "'Mohawk Trail' Easier to Make than It Looks." *Chicago Tribune*, 9 August: 23.

——. 1933c. "Here's another pretty addition to star quilts." *Chicago Tribune*, 10 August: 15.

——. 1933d. "Many Paths Quilt Changes its Name; Oriental in Tone." *Chicago Tribune*, 18 December: 21.

——. 1933e. "Out of Ancient Egypt Comes Gay Design for Modern Quilt." *Chicago Tribune*, 20 August: D3.

——. 1934. "Adventurer's Coin Forms Inspiration of Unusual Quilt." *Chicago Tribune*, 7 April: 21.

——. 1935. "'Oriental Poppy': Is Quilt Showing Modern Harmony." *Chicago Tribune*, 29 April: 14.

——. 1936a. "Simple Quilt Has 'Formosa Fan' As Attractive Theme." *Chicago Tribune*, 20 August: 15.

——. 1936b. "Quilt Pattern is Popular One in Rural Districts." *Chicago Tribune*, 28 March: 19.

——. 1943. "Fan Design for Quilt." *Chicago Tribune*, 13 April: 23.

Caher, Marion. 1931. "Party Treat." *Ladies Home Journal*, January: 13.

Cook, Jesse B. 1931. "San Francisco's Old Chinatown." *San Francisco Police and Peace Officers' Journal*, June. From the Virtual Museum of the City of San Francisco: http://www.sfmuseum. org/hist9/cook.html (accessed 28 March, 2006).

Designs Worth Doing. 1930. "Table Mats in Chinese Design." *Designs Worth Doing 1930–31*. Independence, MO: McKim Studios, p. 15.

——. 1930. "A Beautiful Persian Monogram." *Designs Worth Doing 1930–31*. Independence, MO: McKim Studios, p. 13.

——. 1930. "Chinese Appliqué Towels." *Designs Worth Doing 1930–31*. Independence, MO: McKim Studios, p. 4.

——. 1930. "Easily Applied Painting Designs." *Designs Worth Doing 1930–31*. Independence, MO: McKim Studios, p. 8.

——. 1931a. "Chinee Phone Pad." *Designs Worth Doing 1930–31*. Independence, MO: McKim Studios, p. 37.

——. 1931b. "Oriental Poppy." *Designs Worth Doing: Fall and Winter Catalogue, 1931–32*. Independence, MO: McKim Studios, p. 18.

——. 1931c. "Charming Dollies from Japan." *Designs Worth Doing, Fall and Winter Catalogue 1931–32*. Independence, MO: McKim Studios, p. 33.

Godley, Michael R. 1994. "The End of the Queue: Hair as Symbol in Chinese History." In Geremie R. Barme (ed.) *East Asian History (Vol. 8)*. Canberra: Institute of Advanced Studies, Australian National University, pp. 53–72.

Gunn, Virginia. 1991. "Quilts for Milady's Boudoir." In Laurel Horton (ed.) *Uncoverings 1989*. San Francisco: American Quilt Study Group, pp. 81–101.

Hall, Carrie and Rose Kretsinger. 1935. *The Romance of the Patchwork Quilt in America*. New York: Bonanza Books.

Hing, Bill Ong. 1993. *Making and Remaking Asian America through Immigration Policy, 1850–1990*. Stanford: Stanford University Press.

Hope Winslow's Quilt Book. 1933a. "A Quilt Created by Own Hands Becomes a Greater Treasure as the Years Roll On." *Hope Winslow's Quilt Book*. DesMoines: Home Art Studios, p. 9.

——. 1933b. "Gay Swinging Lantern Quilt." *Hope Winslow's Quilt Book*. DesMoines: Home Art Studios, p. 12.

——. 1933c. "Early American Quilts Are First in Favor Today." *Hope Winslow's Quilt Book*. DesMoines: Home Art Studios, p. 13.

International Quilt Study Center (IQSC), University of Nebraska-Lincoln, accession number 1997.007.0225.

——. 1997.007.0366.

——. 1997.007.0432.

——. 1997.007.0857.

——. 2000.007.0058.

——. 2003.003.0141.

Kim, Hae Jeon and Marilyn R. DeLong. 1992. "Sino-Japanism in Western Women's Fashionable Dress in Harper's Bazar, 1890–1927." *Clothing and Textiles Research Journal* 11(1): 24-30.

Kansas City Star. Date unknown. "For Your Oriental Luncheon." *Kansas City Star*: page unknown.

——. 1933a. "The Pines of Japan." *Kansas City Star*, 11 October: page unknown.

——. 1933b. "The Sacred Mountain in Japanese Motif." *Kansas City Star*, 11 October: page unknown.

——. 1934. "A Japanese Garden." *Kansas City Star*, 8 August: page unknown.

——. 1938. "An Old Pattern with a New Name." *Kansas City Star*, 13 July: page unknown.

Ladies Home Journal. 1925a. "A Fitting Climax to the Perfect Dinner." Advertisement for Jell-O brand gelatin, *Ladies Home Journal*, October: 114.

——. 1925b. "Let Kodak Save the Day." Advertisement for Kodak

Cameras. *Ladies Home Journal,* July: 120.

——. 1925c. "Beauty from Trees." Advertisement for Palmolive soap, *Ladies Home Journal*, July: 45.

Lee, Robert G. 1999. *Orientals: Asian Americans in Popular Culture*. Philadelphia: Temple University Press.

Marchetti, Gina. 2004. "From Fu Manchu to *M. Butterfly* and *Irma Vep*: Cinematic Incarnations of Chinese Villainy." In Murray Pomerance (ed.), *Bad: Infamy, Darkness, Evil, and Slime on Screen*. Albany, NY: State University of New York.

McCall Needlework and Decorative Arts. 1927a. "Modern Needlework and Old Time Patchwork." *McCall Needlework and Decorative Arts*, Spring: 49.

——. 1927b. "Dainty Lingerie Creations for Intimate Wear." *McCall Needlework and Decorative Arts*, Spring 1927: 21.

——. 1927c. "The Fashionable Designs for Painting." *McCall Needlework and Decorative Arts*, Spring: 29.

Mirken, Alan (ed.). 1970. *1927 Edition of the Sears, Roebuck Catalogue*. New York: Crown Publishers, Inc.

Sears and Roebuck. 1930."Stylish Japanese Lounging Garments." 1930. *Sears and Roebuck Catalogue, Fall/Winter 1930–31.* Chicago: Sears and Roebuck Company, p, 348.

Stevens, E. Marion. 1931. "Suggestions for Summer Bazaars or Bridge Parties." *Needlecraft—The Magazine of Home Arts*: 9 (issue number and page extent unknown).

Woman's Home Companion. 1928. "Pillows Are Popular." *Woman's Home Companion*, November: 67.

Woodard, Thomas and Greenstein, Blanche. 1981. *Crib Quilts and Other Small Wonders*. New York: Dutton.

Symbolic Consumption: Dressing for Real and Imagined Space

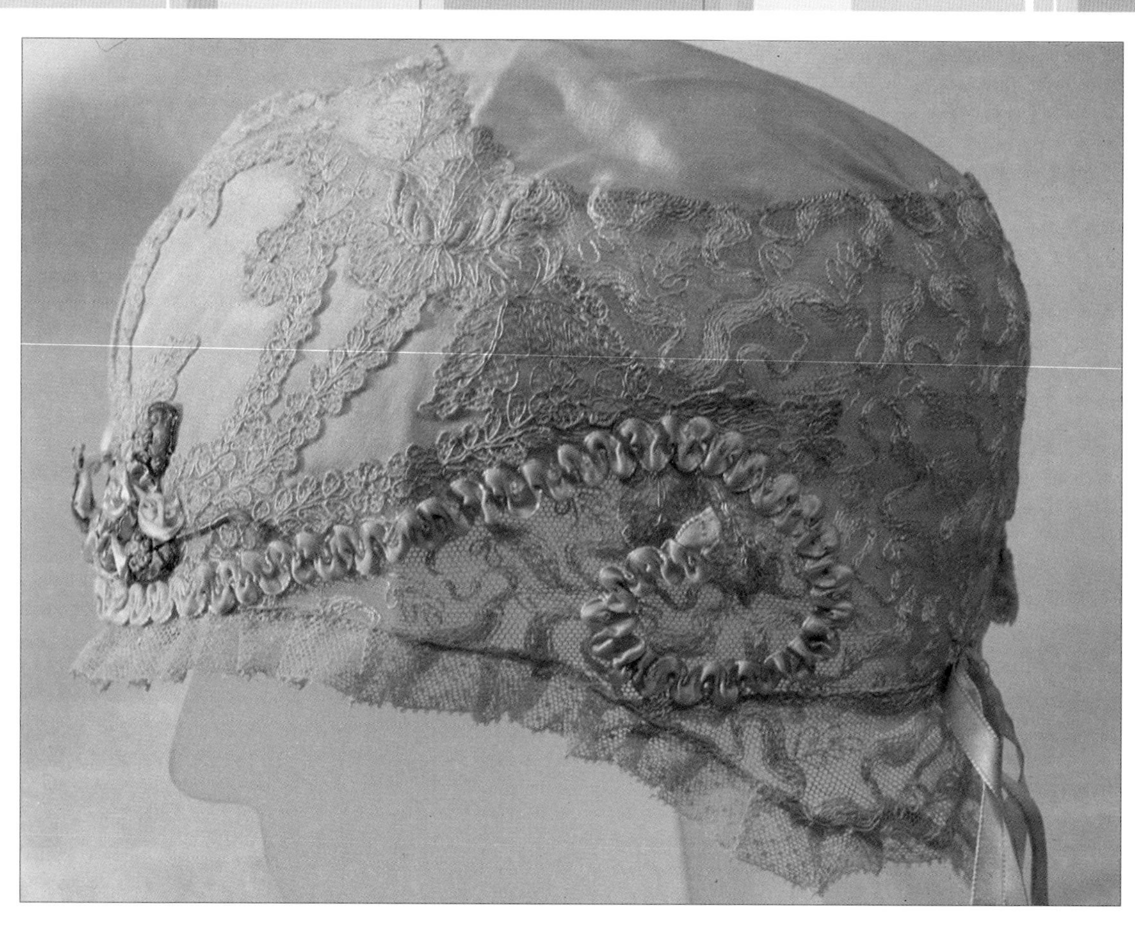

Abstract

The boudoir cap had a lifespan of about fifty years, arising as a distinct dress expression in the last decades of the nineteenth century, encompassing an era of radical change in the social roles and expectations of women in New Zealand. During this time evolving styles reflected these variations, and can be understood both as expressions of the culture that created them and also as tools in the negotiation of new realities. The boudoir cap was worn by women in the boudoir, a lady's private space within the home, to which only intimates were admitted. The actual boudoir was a luxury enjoyed by only a minority of Dunedin women, but boudoir caps were worn by many women, so that through the boudoir cap the concept of the boudoir was available to all as symbolic consumption. Originating in the tradition of covering the hair, the caps were strongly associated with the conventions of modesty and control of sexuality. The boudoir cap was instrumental in the construction of the feminine ideal, and reflects changes in this ideal over time. This paper studies the material culture of the boudoir caps in the Otago Museum collection.

ELAINE WEBSTER

Elaine Webster has recently completed her PhD in Clothing and Textile Sciences, University of Otago, New Zealand, where she has also taught social aspects of dress. She has studied implications of same dressing for identity construction in adolescence through the history and practice of school uniforms in New Zealand.

Textile, Volume 4, Issue 2, pp. 164–183
Reprints available directly from the Publishers.
Photocopying permitted by licence only.

Symbolic Consumption: Dressing for Real and Imagined Space

Introduction

The boudoir cap had a lifespan of about fifty years, arising as a distinct dress expression in the last decades of the nineteenth century, encompassing an era of radical change in the social roles and expectations of women in New Zealand. During this time evolving styles reflected these changes, and can be understood both as expressions of the culture that created them and as tools in the negotiation of new realities. This negotiation took place through symbolic consumption, where dressing for an imaginary boudoir was a rehearsal for an idealized lifestyle in a prosperous and mobile society.

Symbolic consumption is an aspect of consumption, which is what a consumer does through the selection, purchase and use of material objects. Material objects have more than utilitarian and commercial value—they carry and communicate cultural meaning. *The Concise Oxford Dictionary* (2001) defines a symbol as "a thing that represents or stands for another thing, especially a material object representing something abstract." Symbolism is the "use of symbols to represent ideas or qualities," thus symbolic meaning. Symbolic properties of objects are the meanings that objects hold for people, such as the symbolic property of status. As McCracken (1990) suggests, there is often a gap between the real and the ideal in social and personal life. The individual, dreaming of an idealized version of life, comes to see that lifestyle symbolized in an object, so the object becomes a bridge to the attainment of that ideal. This object can serve as proof that the ideal exists, and allows the rehearsal "of a much larger set of possessions, attitudes, circumstances and opportunities" (McCracken 1990: 110). Symbolic consumption then is the consumption in the abstract of an ideal, via the concrete possession and use of a thing that symbolizes that ideal. We appropriate goods to appropriate new status. It seems boudoir caps operated in this way for Otago women.

Boudoir caps were supposedly worn by women in the boudoir—a lady's private space within the home to which only intimates were admitted (Picken 1973). The actual boudoir was a luxury enjoyed by only a minority of New Zealand women, if any, but it seems that boudoir caps were widely worn. Certainly they have survived as artifacts, and there are over fifty in the Otago Museum collection. Why did women wear them? What did they mean? And what was the boudoir?

The word *boudoir* comes to us from the French *bouder*: to pout.

In seventeenth-century France the boudoir was a new type of private space for women "a tiny recess, a very narrow *cabinet* near the chamber one occupies, for pouting unseen when in a bad mood" (Pardailhé-Galabrun 1991: 63–4). The boudoir was a small private room used by the woman of the house for privacy and devotion to her personal affairs away from all the comings and goings of the household. If a woman had no boudoir, then she had to make do with the bedroom, which was seen as her room anyway. The boudoir was not a dressing room or a bathroom, but usually communicated with the master bedroom (Muthesius 1979 [1904, 1908]). There is an essentially feminine and intimate quality to the boudoir, so it is not surprising that a certain eroticism has come to be associated with this space.

A boudoir in France is one thing, but a boudoir in Otago is another. Otago is a province in the lower half of the South Island of New Zealand, an island nation first populated by East Polynesians over 1,000 years ago, and colonized by Britain during the nineteenth century. Planned colonial settlement of Otago began in 1848, and many immigrants were Scottish Presbyterians, who came expressly to found a community based on principles of Scottish piety, independence, and industry. The influence of these pioneers dominated the moral and social life of Otago in the nineteenth century and accounts for much of its historic character (Olssen 1984).

The Otago gold rush in the 1860s dramatically increased both population and prosperity of the province, and made many Otago families wealthy. However, the rapid influx of young single men threatened the moral order (Olssen 1984). Calls for temperance were made by Otago women, mixed with demands for the franchise, equal pay, and the abolition of prostitution and the sexual double standard (Olssen 1984; Dalziel 1986). Their claims were based on an ideal of women as caretakers of social purity and the domesticators of men through their influence in the home. This was also the rationale behind establishing secondary school education for girls, admission to the university, and eventually gaining the right to vote (Olssen 1984; Dalziel 1986). Although the prosperity of Otago was not to last, evidence of its former glory can be seen in the architecture of Dunedin, the main urban center of the province. Evidence also exists in museum collections held in the Otago Museum including the collection of boudoir caps.

The historic dress collection of Otago Museum in Dunedin, New Zealand includes fifty-three boudoir caps, classified as such by various registrars over time and kept together as a discrete collection. Their grouping indicates differences from other caps in the museum collection, such as day caps or sleeping caps, and while such classification may be open to question it nevertheless forms the basis of the current analysis. Like all artifacts, these boudoir caps were subjected to cultural interpretation from the outset. I was asked to study the caps and make a selection to go into an exhibition on nightclothes and underwear, and to find out something about when, where, and why they were worn. The study was conducted using material culture methods (Fleming 1982; Prown 1988), developed specifically for the study of dress artifacts (Severa and Horswill 1989). These methods were further adapted for my own use. The work of Grant McCracken was of particular value at the stage of interpretation. As material culture study begins with close examination of the artifacts and proceeds from there to secondary sources through to interpretation, I began with the caps themselves then went to secondary sources. A range of textual and pictorial sources were used, including dress history, architectural history, New Zealand history, archived magazine and newspaper advertisements and features, and archived house plans and directories. Houses were also visited and people were inter-viewed. An outstanding feature of these caps has been their peripheral nature—they appear in various visual sources and they have survived in collections, yet there is very little direct reference to them, so that much of what I have learned is based on inference. It was however possible to place them within a New Zealand and European hat wearing tradition and to interpret something of their expressive and mediating functions specific to the Otago and New Zealand colonial context.

Fashion and dress are important tools in expressing and restricting social movement, helping to both maintain order and to challenge it. As such fashion can be understood as instrumental, both expressing and mediating change. Their changing styles over time clearly reflect the changing fashions of hats, hairstyles, underwear and nightclothes, but also the changing roles of women. Boudoir caps are interesting artifacts, but become truly fascinating when they are allowed to speak of the culture that created them.

Selection

The collection includes caps in varying styles, materials, methods of construction, age and provenance. Each cap in the collection was examined and general observations made. Following examination, a range of types was defined. Caps were grouped into these types, and one or two selected that best represented that type *and* were suitable for exhibition. Thirteen caps were selected, and these formed the basis of all subsequent analysis. These caps were examined closely and detailed descriptions made, museum reference numbers recorded, photographs taken, then they were set aside for inclusion in the upcoming exhibition. Information was obtained from museum records, including some details of provenance, dates, usually a brief description, and in some instances the wearer of the cap had been identified by the donor. These names provided some important clues, and at a later stage were followed up through local archives and directories.

Many of the caps in the collection were handmade, although some of the later caps incorporated machine sewing. A certain uniformity of cut and construction could be seen in several of the latter, suggesting mass production. Boudoir caps making an appearance in local advertisements were not offered for sale as other items were, so provided no clues about the extent to which they were commercially produced in New Zealand. Mail-order catalogs, another important source for dress historians, were not a feature of clothing retail in New Zealand at that time. The boudoir caps in this collection were more likely to have been purchased from a department store, commissioned from a milliner, or made by the wearer. During the 1870s and 1880s the first clothing factories and retail stores were established in Dunedin, following the trend to mass production (although on a smaller scale) that also characterized clothing production in USA and Europe at that time (Malthus and Brickell 2003). Dressmakers, tailors and milliners also produced clothing on a much smaller scale in either dressmaking shops or as outworkers, and some worked in the client's or their own homes. Many of the new department stores in Dunedin also manufactured the goods they sold. By 1901, over a quarter of Dunedin's workforce worked in the clothing industry, 80 percent of them women, and it is likely their skills were also useful in the home economy, where one or more family members would make items for the family (Malthus and Brickell 2003).

Secondary Sources

There are few textual references to boudoir caps in either contemporary or academic sources, although pictures of boudoir caps did appear in some magazines and advertisements and some dress historians have made passing references to them. Mary Brooks Picken in *The Fashion Dictionary* (1973) defined boudoir caps as being supposedly worn by women in the boudoir, which she also defined as a lady's private space within the home, to which only intimates were admitted. A second, rather narrow definition of the boudoir cap refers to the function of protecting the hairstyle while dressing (O'Hara Callan 1998). On a more sophisticated note, a 1920s *Vogue* article recommended the boudoir cap as being insurance against the great crime of being ugly in bed, going even further to promise that any woman contriving to wear both a new boudoir cap and her best smile, could charm her husband into signing checks virtually against his will (quoted in Probert 1981). From these definitions and descriptions the boudoir cap emerges as having several functions and meanings.

Not surprisingly, photographs of actual wear could not be found, as caps were associated with undress and the bedchamber. Some early twentieth-century newspapers and magazines available in New Zealand contained pictures of boudoir caps, including the sketch and instructions for making "a little cap to match the cami knickers" as a gift idea in the Australasian edition of Weldon's *Ladies Home Journal*, Christmas 1926. Another source was *Mary Card's Book of Things to Wear in Crochet* published in Australia in 1924. This provided patterns for making various styles of boudoir caps in crotchet, accompanied by photographs of models wearing end results. The photographs look rather more ordinary than the glamour drawings usually seen in advertising.

Although some idea of wear practices can be inferred from advertising, and many existing images and analysis from this source have been reproduced in specialized dress histories (such as Ewing 1978), such inference is not without its problems. One problem is that contradictions occur in the ways imagery is interpreted, both now and in the past. Many reproductions only show boudoir caps incidental to the main theme, often an advertisement for glamorous underwear. Although advertising may be primarily concerned with constructing future consumption practices, it may simultaneously reflect something of existing practices and ideals; but as it is hard to know where to draw the line, such sources must be used with caution. From such drawings we can infer that boudoir caps are part of the state of undress, worn in privacy but still intended to be seen, presumably by someone else present in the bedchamber, dressing room, or boudoir, someone likely to be the real or anticipated husband/lover. This interpretation contrasts with the photographs already mentioned and also an advertisement from *The Mirror* in 1928 which shows a cap worn by a nursing mother in her bed while she drinks her health-giving Ovaltine. These are hardly images of glamorous sexuality, and are also confusing because the cap is worn as a night cap. Was "boudoir cap" just a fancy name for a night cap?

The artifacts themselves refuted this, as had the museum registrars who in the past had made (usually) clear distinctions between night caps and boudoir caps. I returned again and again to the caps themselves as touchstones for this work, attempting to evaluate the nature and the meaning of these distinctions. They certainly seemed to be more than "just a night cap" and there really did seem to be something in the name.

Origins

Originating in the tradition of covering the hair, early boudoir caps were associated with the conventions of modesty and the control of sexuality. Nineteenth-century European women always dressed their hair and generally wore head coverings, as a mark of decency, sobriety, and respectability (McDowell 1992). This practice also had the practical function of protecting the hair or hairstyle from the evils of disarray and dirt. One definition of the boudoir cap refers to the function of protecting the hairstyle while dressing (O'Hara Callan 1998). Caps were probably also useful for protecting hairstyles while sleeping; certainly scarves were later used for this.

The earliest caps in the collection are reminiscent of the bonnet in shape, with a ruffle framing the face. Beautifully executed in fine lace, embroidery and hand stitching, the early caps speak of delicacy, finesse, and modesty, and conjure images of women in quiet and genteel labor, women with sufficient time to devote to their production (Figure 1). The important pioneer virtues of industry and skill are evident in these early caps. These early caps are very like the day caps of the 1860s and 1870s and although they were classified as boudoir caps in the museum record, it may be better to consider them as precursors of the boudoir cap. They would certainly have been worn in the more intimate and private sphere of home, and perhaps the corset was also set aside and looser garments worn, allowing a degree of comfort and informality.

After the austerity of pioneer years, Victorian times in New Zealand were characterized by a "relentless pursuit of comfort and material wealth" (Salmond 1986). Home ownership was the ambition of most colonists, and the villas of the affluent middle class were bedecked with the symbols of prosperity and progress. The home came to be seen as a "unique statement and

Figure 1
Early boudoir cap: Limerick lace bonnet, hand-sewn. G92.140 Norman Fitzgerald Collection, Otago Museum.

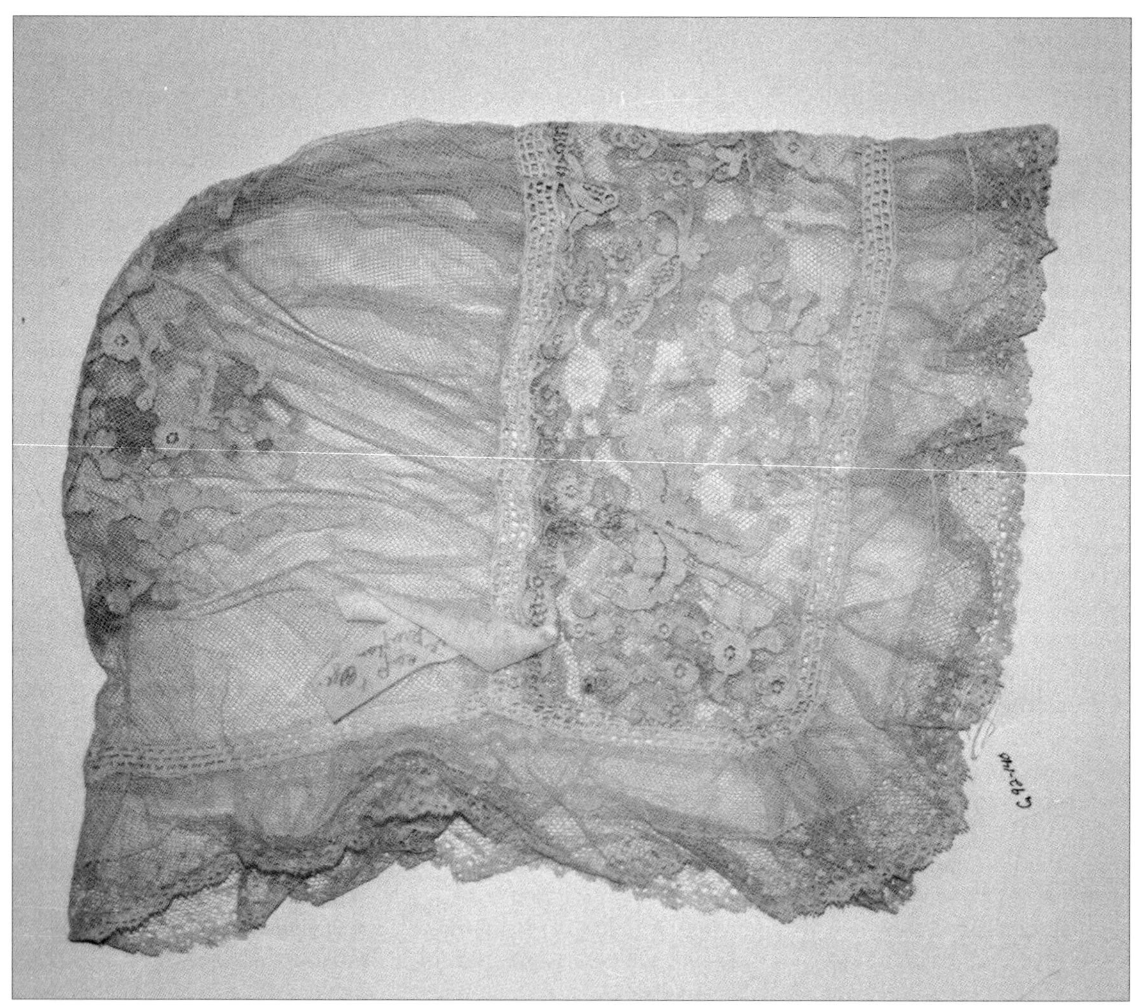

expression of personal taste" and women were expected to be idealistic and self-expressive by nature, and to demonstrate this in their dress and in their homes (Salmond 1986). Books were a source of instruction in correct taste, for example the Art at Home series published by Macmillan of London. One of this series was *Bedroom and Boudoir* by Lady Barker, published in 1878. It is full of decorating tips, health advice, and repeated pleas for harmony in color, pattern and furnishing. Lady Barker was well traveled, and in *Bedroom and Boudoir* she refers to her New Zealand sojourn. She also published an account of her New Zealand experience, so it is very likely she was known and read in the colony. Nowhere in *Bedroom and Boudoir* does Lady Barker clarify the distinction between bedroom and boudoir, instead giving the impression that the name "boudoir" signifies a kind of *attitude* to the bedroom which lifts it into a realm of taste and harmony, informing the choice of furnishings as well as the way in which the space is occupied.

By the turn of the century hair was still being covered but was no longer obscured, and through the first decade, hairstyles increased in volume and height (Clark 1982). Hats were huge, and seemed unrelated to the head, the shape of which was hidden by the hairstyle. During this era, all manner of underwear and nightwear were trimmed in lace, frills, and embroidery, in an exaggerated and erotic femininity (Probert 1981). Boudoir caps dated to this period are trimmed accordingly, and while still covering the hair they suggest

a state of undress, a condition that may lead to sexual intimacy (Steele 1999). These boudoir caps were meant to be seen, presumably by a woman's husband or lover, so may be interpreted as an expression of sexual desire which through the combination of eroticism and modesty preserved respectability (Fields 2002). While the idea of seeing women in their underwear may have been erotic and the invasion of her private space (the boudoir) "a tantalizing crossover from tart to bourgeoisie" (Steele 1999: 462) the private and public interpretations of women's sexuality were scarcely to be framed in those terms.

In New Zealand as elsewhere, women were understood as vital to the maintenance of virtue, morals and manners, and in the colony the parameters of female and male behavior were rigidly drawn (Dalziel 1986; Levesque 1986). Women's sexuality was firmly linked to motherhood and any expressions of sexuality without the risk of pregnancy were seen as deviant, while prostitution and illegitimate births were harshly condemned (Levesque 1986). Even so, in New Zealand in 1913 almost two-thirds of first births to mothers under the age of twenty-one occurred within seven months of marriage, vividly demonstrating the gap between public morals and private practice (Levesque 1986). Although in nineteenth-century New Zealand marriage and motherhood had been the career of most women and sexuality relegated to whores, by the early decades of the twentieth century this was changing.

In an article published in *The Mirror*, a New Zealand newspaper, in 1928, womanhood was defined for the modern girl as controlling the powerful forces of sexual passion (Mcfadden 1928). This passion was defined as essentially selfish pleasure that must be tamed for the nobler purpose of continuing the race, with swift retribution promised for the failure to choose this. Sexual purity was described as a treasure to be guarded in order to secure the richer joys of loving, in particular the special pleasure of motherhood, sacrifices notwithstanding. Even so, the writer acknowledged the desires of modern girls to have power over men, the power of charm and sexual attraction (Mcfadden 1928). Dress (and undress) is instrumental in this sexual and attractive power and has long been exploited for this purpose (Ribeiro 1986; Steele 1999). There are also wider links between the caps and the supposed sexual freedom of the New Woman or La Garçonne with her short hair, new wage earning power, and dangerous independence (Zdatny 1997; Stansell 2000).

There are several examples of the classic Edwardian style in the collection (Figure 2). Their shape is derived from the mob cap, with crocheted netting over white tulle finished in delicately scalloped edges to create the lacy and fragile texture so favored in this era. The ruffle, though narrower, still frames the face. There are several caps of similar materials and construction, suggesting that it was popular style, and perhaps patterns were available. With minimal expense a transformation could be made—from head covering to boudoir cap, private domain to boudoir, restraint and modesty to glamorous sexuality. This was a radical departure from a female sexuality entirely linked to reproductive function (Brookes 1986).

During these years there were radical changes in the physical and social worlds of New Zealand women. Having achieved the right to vote in 1893 on the basis of their role in the home, the franchise affirmed and upheld their domestic and maternal roles and had a "strangling effect" on the expansion of their roles in society (Dalziel 1986). However, women increasingly participated in paid employment and public life, and participation in sports also increased, challenging social conventions defining the female body and where she could go (Page 1998). Favored sports were tennis and bicycle riding (Figure 3). The advent of moving pictures may also have provided alternative ideals and aspirations. Increased prosperity coupled with government intervention to promote spending on housing, gave women increased consumer power and choices (Petersen 2001).

Rapid and profound changes took place in the lives of New Zealand women in the first three decades of the twentieth century, in work patterns, family size, transportation, leisure and dress (Malthus and Brickell 2003). Fashion leapt to a new era of simplicity and modernity. For the first time, women en masse cut their hair short, symbolically bringing their sexuality under their own control (Zdatny 1997; Smith 1998). The cloche hats of the period fitted the head, and

Figure 2
Edwardian boudoir cap: crochet over tulle, hand-sewn. F79.610 Presented by Mrs. W.T. McMillan, Otago Museum.

Figure 3
Bicycles at St Clair Beach, Dunedin, 1909. Hocken Library, Uare Taoka o Hakena, University of Otago.

the streamlined head became a thing of beauty in itself (Clark 1982). Mrs. Macdonald of Dunedin owned some of the most elaborate and modern boudoir caps in the collection (Figure 4). She lived in High Street, Dunedin, with her husband, Dr. Robert Gordon Macdonald during the 1920s (Stones 1926). Her house, since converted into flats, is unlikely to have had either a dressing room or a boudoir.

From about the 1920s the practice arose of both sexes pottering around the house in pajamas, partly due to the new indoor bathrooms and also changing attitudes to the body and sexuality, breaking down the privacy of bedclothes (Willet and Cunnington 1981). At this time the boudoir cap really came into its own, and appears in magazine advertisements and in pattern books. The second edition of *Mary Card's Book of Things to Wear in Crochet* was published in Melbourne in 1924, and was available in New Zealand. It shows pictures of "dainty" boudoir caps and provides full instructions for making them (Figure 5).

The new styles were variations of the cloche and often included an emphasis on the ears. The ruffle was replaced with a band around the brow, softened as always by a lace or scalloped edge. Many were trimmed in ribbon work, machine lace, and combinations of lace and silk or crepe (Figure 6). They were delicate, fragile, and elaborate. These caps truly belonged in the boudoir, but they were also distinctly for young and wealthy women. They indicated a retreat to a delicate interior life, a life of leisure, beauty, and decoration. Many of these later caps appeared to be commercially produced, no longer the product of taste, skill and industry in the home. The virtue of feminine taste

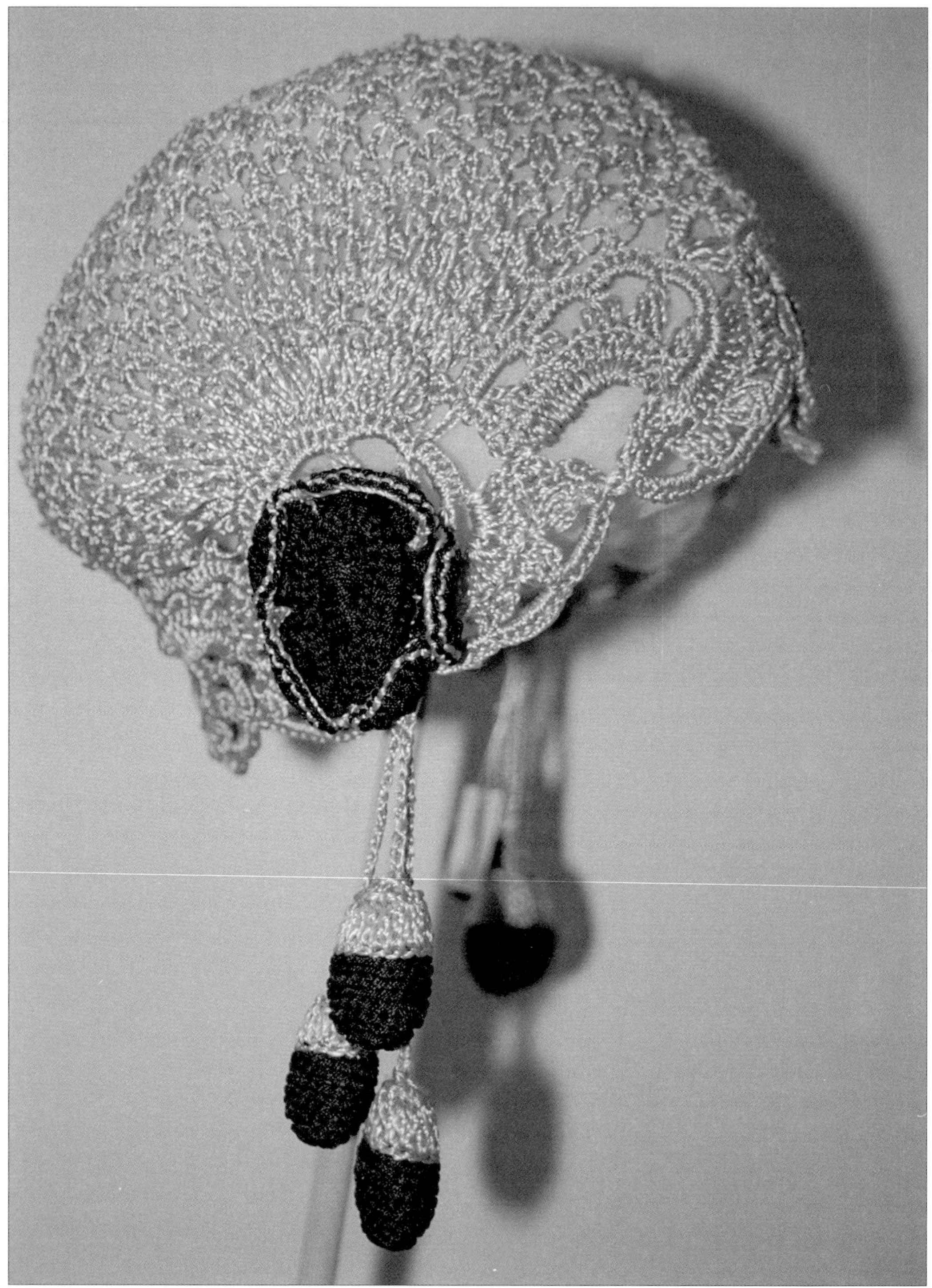

Figure 4
Cloche-style boudoir cap: crocheted rayon yarn in orange and black. G85.706 Otago Museum.

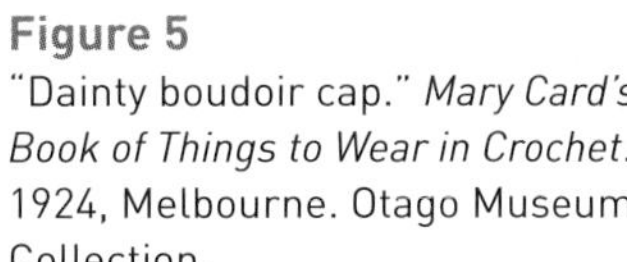

Figure 5
"Dainty boudoir cap." *Mary Card's Book of Things to Wear in Crochet.* 1924, Melbourne. Otago Museum Collection.

was expressed as consumer choice instead.

A number of caps in the collection were fashionable in the late 1920s. Several belonged to Mrs. Zealandia Iverach, donated to the museum collection by her niece Mrs. Service. Mrs. Iverach was a daughter of Sir John Ross, who had emigrated from Scotland in 1861 and achieved great wealth with his importing and manufacturing business. His children grew up on the large family property in Newington Avenue, and his daughters attended finishing school in Switzerland, unusual in New Zealand (Galer 1995; Strachan 1998). At his death in 1927 Sir John left an estate worth over quarter of a million pounds, having been one of New Zealand's most successful businessmen. During the 1930s Dr. and Mrs. Iverach built a large house on her portion of the Newington Avenue property (Galer 1995; Thomson 1998). This house has five bedrooms and several small dressing rooms, and a very pleasant sun porch connects the main bedroom with a guest room, but there is no boudoir.

While New Zealand did not have a class structure in the sense of Britain or Europe, there were differences among people based on economic resources that divided people in similar ways. The majority of British immigrants to New Zealand during the nineteenth century were working class people, but many had managed to advance themselves, to buy land, establish businesses, and to prosper in the colony (Salmond 1986). Some

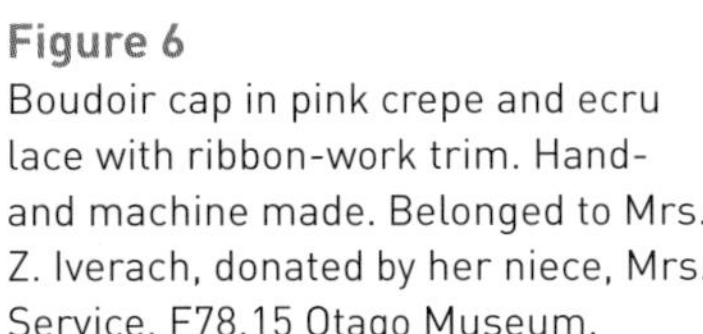

Figure 6
Boudoir cap in pink crepe and ecru
lace with ribbon-work trim. Hand-
and machine made. Belonged to Mrs.
Z. Iverach, donated by her niece, Mrs.
Service. F78.15 Otago Museum.

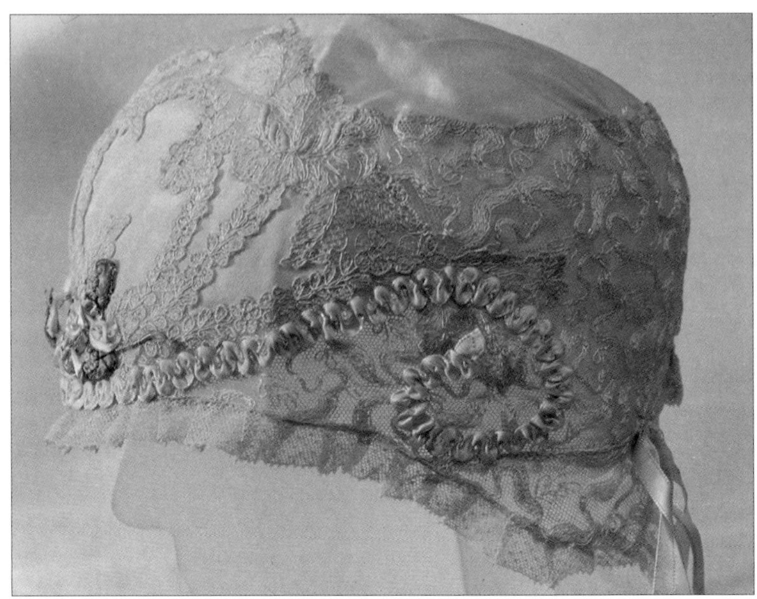

had done very well, and it was the
preoccupation of many to better
themselves. These later caps
belonged to women whose families
really did manage this, suggesting
a very different daily experience to
that of other women, most of whom
had no domestic help and many
of whom were working to support
their families (Dalziel 1986).

The boudoir caps speak so
strongly of leisure and decoration,
especially the later ones, there is
little to connect them to working
class lives. This brings us to
the final cap considered in this
study (Figure 7) which was dated
1930s, when New Zealanders
were experiencing a serious
economic depression. It is a crude
interpretation of the mob cap of
earlier times, executed in rather
clumsy stitching and apparently
made up from scraps of material,
with only very simple decorative
treatment. The embroidery

and lace edging make the all
important gesture of decoration,
that recognizable expression of
female identity, and though crude,
this succeeds. It appears to have
been made by someone who was
not a seamstress, but who did
take care to finish all the edges.
This suggests making do, which
brings class issues to mind. The
contrast between this cap and
those from the 1920s could not
be greater. There is a practicality
and functionality to this cap that
completely removes it from any
suggestion of upper class isolation
and the delicate interiors implicit in
those others. But no wonder, times
had changed again.

Two World Wars and the Great
Depression had sapped the
strength from the old ways, and
symbols of class divisions, so
avidly sought before, shifted into
different spheres. The gap between
classes seemed to widen, although

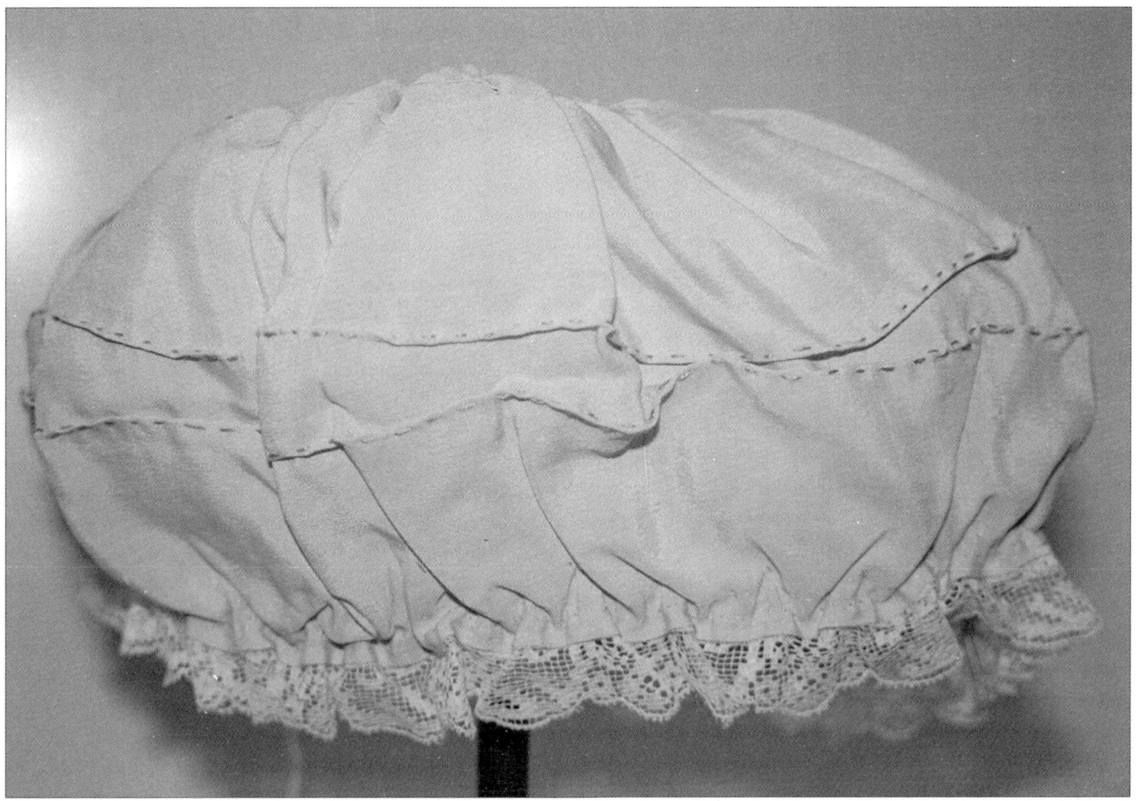

Figure 7
Hand-sewn cap of the 1930s, pink/orange. From Mrs. Lyndall Hancock. G85.699 Otago Museum.

the egalitarian myth persisted (Consedine 1989). Women were still unlikely to appear in public without a hat, but there had been profound changes in the construction of women's public and private lives (Page 1998; Olssen 1999; Brookes, Cooper and Law 2003).

Searching for the Boudoir
But where was the boudoir? Was this just a fancy name for bedroom? In her book *Bedroom and Boudoir* Lady Barker, although making no other distinctions, described the boudoir as a woman's private place to idle and sulk (Barker 1878). But as hardly anybody actually seemed to have a boudoir, we must assume that a boudoir was as much a manner of occupying a space as a space itself. It probably overlapped the bedroom or a corner of it as a kind of ultra-feminized space where a woman dressed her hair and applied what Lady Barker termed the "weapons of beauty" and perhaps turning her back on the room.

Olveston, Dunedin's best claim to a stately home, was built in 1904 for David Theomin and his family, and was opened to the public in 1967 (Figure 8). There is a wonderful dressing room off the master bedroom, but it was used by the man of the house. Their teenage daughter Dorothy had her room divided into bedroom and sitting room where she might entertain one or two friends, but this room was hardly a boudoir.

Museum records and local directories and archives were used to obtain addresses for some of the women whose caps were in the collection; none of these houses had boudoirs. Other house plans were examined in the course of

Figure 8
Olveston: stately home in Dunedin,
built in 1904. Photograph: E. Webster.

this study, including plans held by individual house owners and collections held in the city archives and by Oakley Gray (architects) of Dunedin. The search focused on houses built during the 1920s, the heyday of the boudoir cap. The plans of a house in Claremont Street built in 1919 show a billiard room, sewing room, maid's room, sleeping balcony, four bedrooms, a dressing room, but no boudoir. Another home in Claremont Street built in 1920–21 also had no boudoir, although it did have a darkroom (Figure 9). The word "boudoir" does appear in one plan, that of a house designed by Basil Hooper in 1910 for the Throp family, (brought to my attention by architectural historian Christopher Baughen; the only one he has ever come across). This boudoir is at one end of the large living room, separated only by a curtain which can be drawn back to enlarge the living room, a feature of the house. This "boudoir" also opens into the hallway, so it seems to be a separate sitting room, not the French boudoir nor that described by Lady Barker. There are a few examples of private sitting rooms in Otago homes, but they are not called boudoirs, and they do not connect to the master bedroom. It seems unlikely that the woman of the house would occupy such a room in the semi-dressed state associated with the boudoir cap. The boudoir, in the sense of private and intimate

Figure 9
House in Claremont St., Dunedin built in 1920–21 for the McKellar family. Current owners Paul and Lisa Coghill.
Photograph: E. Webster.

feminine space, could not be found in Dunedin.

Colonial middle and upper class women had vastly different realities to their counterparts in Britain and Europe. Their houses were far less grand, and though they may have been at the pinnacle of New Zealand society, they could never aspire to Continental levels of wealth or influence. They adopted the idea of the boudoir from the continent, perhaps as an ideal of wealth, but while the boudoir cap translated, the boudoir did not. They appropriated the cachet of the boudoir without actually having one. In Otago the boudoir seems to have not been a room at all, but a symbolic space, intensely private, intimate and feminine, and they occupied it symbolically through the boudoir cap. In wearing the boudoir cap they dressed in real space for imagined space.

Although boudoir caps originated in the hat-wearing tradition, the earlier caps had been more about the conventions of modesty and the ways in which women occupied the home. That they were so closely associated with night clothes and the bedchamber affirms their connection with women's sexuality; not even in the privacy of the bedroom did nineteenth-century women seem to abandon their respectability and modesty. Emancipation was first expressed in the Edwardian caps as a flaunting of that sexual power so long suppressed, in an erotic and exaggerated femininity. At the same time, the ruffles, frills and puffs offered an assurance that women did not constitute a threat to the intellectual dominance of men. Not surprisingly, this placating gesture was soon abandoned as women experienced both new freedoms and a harsher reality. New doors opened for ordinary New Zealand women in areas the suffragettes had never anticipated. Many women no longer expected to retreat into the home upon marriage, conducting their affairs from the interior, surrounded in symbols of domesticity, and dependent on their husband's goodwill. Many had jobs and income of their own, and choices that did not always include marriage and motherhood. More and more women cut their hair, visited the hairdresser, engaged in sport, and earned their own money. The boudoir cap could not survive this change.

While boudoir caps had operated more generally as symbols, their final manifestation in fashion was as status symbol among the (newly) wealthy. They became part of the repertoire of class differences, communicating "a system of conceptual differences between social categories," affirming the fulfillment of local ideals among the select few, and serving as proof of the existence of an upper class and of the individual's claim to it (McCracken 1990). Boudoir caps had to some extent been the products of leisure, but the commercially produced caps replaced them with an *impression* of leisure. Women of the upper class were no longer expected to actively produce the objects used in constructing their femininity, they could purchase them instead. They had become decorative without industry. They had arrived.

Dress "…allows us to suppose that while things may not presently conform to ideal expectations, there is a place and time in which they do" (McCracken 1990: 116). Thus dress helps us to remember who we are, but perhaps more importantly, dress assists us in the construction of who we wish to be.

Acknowledgments

Curators Jane Malthus and Moira White, Otago Museum, Dunedin; Hocken Library, Uare Taoka o Hakena, University of Otago, Dunedin; John Gray, Oakley Gray Architects, Dunedin; Bill Sykes, Archivist, Dunedin City Council; Rod Jansen, research assistant; Michael Findlay, design historian; Christopher Baughen, architectural historian; Julie and Tom Whitefield, Newington Ave, Dunedin; Paul and Lisa Coghill, Claremont St.

References

Barker, Lady. 1878. *The Bedroom and Boudoir.* London: Macmillan.

Brookes, B. 1986. "Reproductive Rights: The Debate over Abortion and Birth Control in the 1930s." In B. Brookes, C. Macdonald, and M. Tennant (eds) *Women in History: Essays on European Women in New Zealand.* Wellington: Allen and Unwin/Port Nicholson Press.

Brookes, B., A. Cooper and R. Law (eds). 2003. *Sites of Gender: Women, Men and Modernity in Southern Dunedin, 1890–1939.* Auckland: Auckland University Press.

Card, M. 1924. *Mary Card's Book of Things to Wear in Crochet* (2nd edn). Melbourne: Fitchett Brothers.

Clark, F. 1982. *Hats: The Costume Accessories Series.* London: B.T. Batsford.

Consedine, B. 1989. "Inequality and the Egalitarian Myth." In D. Novitz and B. Willmott (eds) *Culture and Identity in New Zealand.* Wellington: GP Books.

Dalziel, R. 1986. "The Colonial Helpmeet: Women's Role and the Vote in Nineteenth Century New Zealand." In B. Brookes, C. Macdonald, and M. Tennant (eds)

Women in History: Essays on European Women in New Zealand. Wellington: Allen and Unwin/Port Nicholson Press.

Ewing, E. 1978. *Dress and Undress: A History of Women's Underwear*. New York: Drama Book Specialists.

Fields, J. 2002. "Erotic Modesty: (Ad)dressing Female Sexuality and Propriety in Open and Closed Drawers, USA, 1890–1930." *Gender and History* 14(3): 492–515.

Fleming, E. M. 1982. "Artifact study: A Proposed Model." In T. J. Schlereth (ed.) *Material Culture Studies in America*. Nashville, Tennessee: The American Association for State and Local History.

Galer, L. 1995. *Houses of Dunedin*. Dunedin: Allied Press.

Levesque, A. 1986. "Prescribers and Rebels: Attitudes to European Women's Sexuality in New Zealand, 1860–1916." In B. Brookes, C. Macdonald, and M. Tennant (eds) *Women in History: Essays on European Women in New Zealand*. Wellington: Allen and Unwin/Port Nicholson Press.

McCracken, G. 1990. *Culture and Consumption: New Approaches to the Symbolic Character of Consumer Goods and Activities*. Bloomington and Indianapolis: Indiana University Press.

McDowell, C. 1992. *Hats: Status, Style and Glamour*. London: Thames and Hudson.

Mcfadden, B. 1928. "What a Modern Girl Should Know: A Straightforward Talk to Young Women on the Meaning of Womanhood: Its Development and its Supreme Power in Human Life." *The Mirror* (1 October): 16, 20.

Malthus, J. and C. Brickell. 2003. "Producing and Consuming Gender: The Case of Clothing." In B. Brookes, A. Cooper, and R. Law (eds) *Sites of Gender: Women, Men and Modernity in Southern Dunedin, 1890–1939*. Auckland: Auckland University Press.

Muthesius, H. 1979 [1904, 1908]. *The English House*. New York: Rizzoli.

Olssen, E. 1984. *A History of Otago*. Dunedin: John McIndoe Press.

——. 1999. "Families and the Gendering of European New Zealand in the Colonial Period 1840–1880." In C. Daley and D. Montgomerie (eds) *The Gendered Kiwi*. Auckland: Auckland University Press.

O'Hara Callan, G. 1998. *The Dictionary of Fashion and Fashion Designers*. London: Thames and Hudson.

Page, D. 1998. "Hopes fulfilled? Otago women at the end of the Victorian era" in N. J. Bethune (ed.) *Work 'n' Pastimes: 150 Years of Pain and Pleasure, Labour and Leisure*. Dunedin: New Zealand Society of Genealogists.

Pardailhé-Galabrun, A. 1991. *The Birth of Intimacy* [English translation] Cambridge: Polity Press.

Pearsall, J. (ed.) 2001. *Concise Oxford Dictionary* (10th edn). Oxford: Oxford University Press.

Petersen, A. K. 2001. *New Zealanders at Home: A Cultural History of Domestic Interiors 1814–1914*. Dunedin: University of Otago Press.

Picken, M. B. 1973. *The Fashion Dictionary*. New York: Funk & Wagnells.

Probert, C. 1981. *Lingerie in Vogue since 1910* London: Thames and Hudson.

Prown, J. D. 1988. "Mind in Matter: An Introduction to Material Culture Theory and Method." In T. J. Schlereth (ed.) *Material Culture Studies in America*. Nashville, TN: The American Association for State and Local History.

Ribeiro, A. 1986. *Dress and Morality*. London: B.T. Batsford.

Salmond, J. 1986. *Old New Zealand Houses 1800–1940*. Auckland: Reed Methuen.

Severa, J. and M. Horswill. 1989. "Costume as Material Culture" *Dress* 15: 51–64.

Smith, C. 1998. *The Business of Beauty: A History of Hairdressers 1920s to 1960s*. Unpublished PhD Thesis, University of Otago.

Stansell, C. 2000. *American Moderns: Bohemian New York and the Creation of a New Century*. New York: Henry Holt.

Steele, V. 1999. "The Corset: Fashion and Eroticism" *Fashion Theory* 3(4): 449–74.

Stones, G.A (ed.). 1926. *Stone's Otago and Southland Directory* [published annually, 1921–40]. Dunedin: Stones and Sons and Co.

Strachan, S. R. 1998. "Ross, John" in J. Thomson (ed.) *Southern People. A Dictionary of Otago and Southland*. Dunedin: Longacre Press.

Willett, C. and P. Cunnington, with revisions by A. D. Mansfield and V. Mansfield. 1981. *The History of Underclothes*. London: Faber and Faber.

Zdatny, S. 1997. "The Boyish Look and the Liberated Woman: The Politics and Aesthetics of Women's Hairstyles." *Fashion Theory* 1 (4): 367–98.

Talk about Muslin: Jane Austen's *Northanger Abbey*

Abstract

Though Jane Austen has few references to dress in her novels, muslin, and talk about muslin, play a significant role in *Northanger Abbey*. Catherine Morland's first conversation with Henry Tilney, the man she eventually marries, is about her sprigged muslin dress and its properties. Austen's point is that clothing can be as appropriate a topic of conversation between men and women as art and literature. But we are also shown how other characters talk less sensibly, more obsessively and even dangerously about clothes.

CLAIR HUGHES

Clair Hughes, educated in Scotland and at the Courtauld Institute, London, taught Art History and English Literature in Britain and Japan, Now retired in France, she is working on the usage of dress in novels. She has published a book and articles on Henry James, and a book on dress in the eighteenth and nineteenth-century novel, *Dressed in Fiction* (2005), published by Berg.

Textile, Volume 4, Issue 2, pp. 184–197
Reprints available directly from the Publishers.
Photocopying permitted by licence only.

Talk about Muslin: Jane Austen's *Northanger Abbey*

Sarah Byng, the heroine of one of Hilaire Belloc's *Cautionary Tales for Children*, refuses to learn to read, and subsequent events confirm her "instinctive guess / That Literature breeds distress." The debate about the propriety of novel-reading for young women, while looking comic at the end of the nineteenth century, was a very real worry one hundred years before. If Arabella, the heroine of Charlotte Lennox's novel, *The Female Quixote* of 1752, had contented herself with the usual female occupations of "Dressing, Dancing and Tattling over Tea-tables" and not devoured French romances and dressed herself like a fictional heroine, she might happily have accepted marriage and a life of insignificance, and not longed for the adventures that get her into such trouble. Arabella's reading, however, frees her to imagine worlds beyond her own dull one and this lends a complex, even proto-feminist aspect to her character—Sarah Byng was, after all, as Belloc tells us, "a most uncultured gal" (Belloc 1968 [1907] 61: 58).

Catherine Morland, heroine of Jane Austen's 1798 novel, *Northanger Abbey*, although another enthusiastic romance-reader, has been poorly educated, unlike Arabella. Her naïve imagination has been fed by the novels of Ann Radcliffe, a contemporary of Austen's, whose gothic romances—*The Mysteries of Udolpho, The Romance of the Forest*, and *The Italian*—were best-sellers. Mrs Radcliffe's heroines are beautiful, pure and persecuted. These young and unprotected women, fleeing through landscapes of ruined castles, dense forests, towering mountains and bottomless ravines, were subject to multiple threats. Murder, incest, concealed passages, supernatural phenomena, wicked nuns, monks and uncles ensure that no Radcliffe heroine ever has a decent night's sleep nor a moment to change her dress—which was nonetheless invariably becoming (especially when disarrayed) and usually white. In the interests of credibility, everything in her novels was vague: the setting was southern European—such horrors only being possible in Catholic countries—and the period sixteenth or seventeenth century. Dress details in Radcliffe's novels were therefore sketchy, with an occasional slashed sleeve to provide historical color, or a cloak for disguise. Veils, however, were in constant use and there was a particularly exciting one in Catherine's favorite, *The Mysteries of Udolpho*.

Despite the length of Radcliffe's novels and their extensive descriptions of scenery and buildings, there is little interest in dress. Anne Hollander has noted that the design of garments, and the way they look when worn, is nearly always missing from the "literary mirror" (Hollander 1993 [1975]: 419) when held up to nature; it is a pre-existent image assumed by the author to be familiar to the reader. Dress is invoked principally in connection with dramatic conditions or actions—disarrayed gowns or noisy amour in Radcliffe's novels, for example. Action in these novels is all externalized, and so hectic that the underpinnings of normality have no place at all in the lives of her heroines; only a bed, in which to sink, exhausted, at dawn, seems necessary.

Austen had read and admired Lennox's *The Female Quixote* and we might guess that she found the unstoppable Arabella more entertaining than Radcliffe's girls with their overwrought sufferings. "Run mad as often as you chuse," advises Sophia, on her deathbed, in Austen's juvenile novella, *Love and Friendship*, "but do not faint" (Austen 2000 [1954]: 28). Although *Northanger Abbey* is both a Gothic novel and a parody of one, not a great deal happens to Catherine that could be described as an "adventure," nor (at first) does she have any of the requirements of a heroine—although in leaving her unromantically large family to visit Bath, invited by the wealthy but inadequate Mr and Mrs Allen, she does in fact become vulnerable. Anticipated supernatural thrills and dark crimes, however, never materialize; instead very real threats to Catherine's emotional and even physical wellbeing emerge first from the daily social round in Bath and then in the family life of the Tilneys at Northanger Abbey. It is the effect of these events on the education

of Catherine that concerns Austen, and Catherine's drama is thus more internalized than that of any of Radcliffe's interchangeable heroines.

Compared with Austen's later heroines, Catherine has been criticized for showing little psychological development—she still seems very young and naïve at the end of the novel (Duckworth 1971: 91). She does however undergo a process of enlightenment about herself and others, and in the process she falls in love and finds her love returned. Clothes and the interpretation of their qualities, play their part in this process. Dress was certainly important in Austen's own life, but it has to be said, there are few precise descriptions of dress in the novels. This is not because her heroines are uninterested in dress, but, as Penelope Byrde points out, because dress "was not considered a suitable or interesting topic for general conversation" (Byrde 1999: 13)—and decorum is a key virtue in the novels. It is, therefore, what the characters reveal of themselves when they *talk* about clothes that is significant, rather than their description of styles or fashions. Austen herself discussed dresses, hats, caps, shoes, gloves and petticoats upside down and inside and out—but only in her letters to her family and friends, whose essence is the often quite indecorous trivia of daily life. She seems, as Byrde notes, "to have had a weakness for stockings" (Byrde 1999: 28), especially silk ones. Descriptions of dances, dinner and tea parties play a large part in these letters and the dress of her acquaintance is subject

to a lively, indiscreet and highly critical commentary. When she writes to Cassandra, her sister, she frequently commissions her to buy dress materials and trimmings, or describes those she herself has bought for Cassandra. Changes in fashion are commented upon, usually with a view to altering existing garments—sadly, for most of her life Jane Austen had not the means to fully indulge her love of clothes.

Mrs Allen, of *Northanger Abbey*, has, however, indulged Catherine with a new dress for her first ball in the Bath Assembly Rooms, where Catherine meets Henry Tilney. Bath was now *the* fashionable city of the late eighteenth century; a spa town for health cures and leisure activities, for dancing, gambling and theatre-going. It had lately undergone a frenzied building and rebuilding program and was now an elegant city full of shops for the consuming middle-classes, and of places to display their purchases. One of these arenas for display was the Assembly Rooms, where Henry and Catherine have their first crucial conversation, at the end of which a remark of Henry's makes Catherine giggle—"'How can you … be so—,' she almost said strange" (Austen 1995 [1798]: 26). A rather bold thing for a heroine to say to a hero at their initial meeting, but then he has just had a very odd conversation with Mrs Allen. Mrs Allen's passion, we are told, is dress. The difference between Austen's own passion and Mrs Allen's is that nothing else occupies Mrs Allen's mind, a fault which, Austen warns us, will "tend to promote the general distress of the work" (Austen

1995 [1798]: 18). It *is* "strange," therefore, that a key topic of Henry Tilney's first conversation with Catherine, developed at length in the subsequent exchange with Mrs Allen, is also dress—in this case muslin. In this, as in all Austen's novels, characters, like Mrs Allen, whose conversation runs on clothes and fashion, are not only shown as silly but also morally deficient. Are we then to consider Henry also in a negative light? And what are we to make of the fact that all this talk about muslin for ladies' dresses comes from a young *man*?

Henry starts by making Catherine laugh with his teasing parody of what a young man says to a young woman at a ball, and then imagines how she will record their meeting in her "romantic heroine's journal": "went to the Lower Rooms; wore my sprigged muslin robe with blue trimmings— plain black shoes—appeared to much advantage; but was strangely harassed by a queer half-witted man" (Austen 1995 [1798]: 24). Of course, what Henry has cleverly done is to compliment Catherine on her appearance, but saved his remark from the triteness of standard compliments by self-mockery. He has also crossed the unspoken barrier between male and female worlds in the matter of courtship behavior—young men are not supposed to know that young ladies write about them in their journals. Henry's subsequent exchange with Mrs Allen on the practical aspects of muslin takes his venture into female territory even further.

When Mrs Allen interrupts Henry's and Catherine's conversation, wailing over the torn sleeve of her muslin dress which cost nine shillings a yard, Henry astonishes her by saying "'[t]hat is exactly what I should have guessed it, madam.' 'Do you understand muslins, sir?' 'Particularly well

… my sister has often trusted me in the choice of a gown. I bought one for her the other day, and it was pronounced to be a prodigious bargain by every lady who saw it. I paid but five shillings a yard for it, and a true Indian muslin.'" Mrs Allen is "quite struck" and pursues the topic, asking Henry his opinion of Catherine's muslin gown, "It is very pretty, madam … but I do not think it will wash well; I am afraid it will fray" (Austen 1995 [1798]: 25, 26). He reassures them, however, that muslin is so useful that Catherine will be able to recycle her dress for handkerchiefs or caps. The topic of muslin continues until the dancing starts again, and, as far as Catherine can see, Henry is perfectly polite and serious throughout.

In decoding this conversation from a modern standpoint we must recall that muslins were to the late eighteenth and early nineteenth centuries what synthetic fibers were to the mid-twentieth century—they transformed life. Up to the end of the eighteenth century formal clothing for both men and women, with any claims to prosperity and fashion, were of silk, satin or velvet. Wool or fustian (a coarse linen and cotton mixture) was worn further down the social scale, or for informal, country-wear. Silk or linen lace edged sleeves and necks not only because the touches of white or cream were flattering, but because lace was also washable, whereas the other costlier, heavier materials were not. Muslin is a light, fine, washable cotton, but from 1721 until 1774 cotton textiles had been banned in England, to protect the silk industry. People with money found ways round the legislation, of course, and Indian muslin—which the law excluded—began to be very popular from the 1760s (Ribeiro 1995: 70). After 1774 cotton was imported and cotton cloth manufactured in England, providing the impetus for the enormous growth and eventual dominance of the British textile industry, but real Indian muslin—as Henry Tilney makes clear—had greater chic. The French—for political reasons perhaps—preferred the Indian variety and what was French was, for the rest of Europe, fashionable, despite the Napoleonic Wars.

Muslin was ideally suited to reproducing the draped effects of antique statuary. Whether the increasing popularity of a light and restrained neo-classical style of dress was a result of muslin's special properties, or whether muslin became popular *because* it lent itself so well to this style is a chicken-and-egg question; but certainly by the time Catherine attends her first ball in Bath in the 1790s everyone who can afford it is wearing muslin and this continues to be true well into the next century. In one of her letters, referring to her hopes for a new muslin gown, Austen says she is determined "to buy a handsome one whenever I can, & I am so tired and ashamed of half my present stock, that I even blush at the sight of the wardrobe that

contains them" (Le Faye 1997: 30). Muslin was relatively cheap, but looking at Barbara Johnson's *Album of Fashion and Fabrics*, Mrs Allen's muslin at nine shillings a yard seems overpriced. Barbara Johnson was given nine yards of dark blue figured muslin—a color appropriate for her age—by her brother in 1800, at three shillings and sixpence a yard; sarsenet (a woven silk) of the same period was five shillings a yard; French satin, seven shillings and printed calico, two and sixpence (Rothstein 1987: 52, 55, 39, 45). To Austen's readers, Mrs Allen must have seemed not only a silly woman, an inadequate chaperone but recklessly profligate. In Mrs Allen's defense, it must be said that Miss Johnson, in 1769 when much younger, bought a white sprigged muslin for ten shillings a yard, although this particular muslin was of an unusually generous width (Rothstein, 1987: 13).

Muslin did have the advantage of being easy to work with, therefore feasible for the home-dressmaker, though, as Henry points out, quite fragile. It was thus possible to own more than one muslin dress without straining the budget. But because muslin garments soiled easily and had to be washed and changed often, extensive indulgence in this fashion involved the employment of several servants. A muslin dress, however, could be altered at home and, because it was cotton, it was easier to dye than heavier fabrics. Jane Austen and her sister, both on limited incomes, tended to keep their muslins for special occasions. Jane complains about the poor laundering of a new dress despite

having asked that care should be taken, and she writes of dyeing an old muslin gown a darker color. As they get older the sisters seem to favor the tougher wool and silk mix of bombazine for daily use (Le Faye 1997: 6, 146, 256).

Because muslin was washable, it was possible for the fashionable woman to pursue the analogy with classical statuary even further by favoring white or light pastel colors. When white muslin began its career it was associated with children, but Mrs Allen, we note, as well as Catherine, wears muslin. On the older, plumper figure this sometimes resulted in an unfortunate babyish appearance, an effect that caricaturists of the period, such as Thomas Rowlandson, were quick to exploit—and I suspect Mrs Allen may have fallen into this category. But as we can see in the painting by Rolinda Sharples of *The Cloakroom, Clifton Assembly Rooms*, of 1817 (Figure 1), the general effect of these simple, light-colored gauzy dresses is elegant and flattering to most women, especially when seen against the dark, sharp outlines of formal, male evening wear. The dresses here are a little later than those described in *Northanger Abbey*, and we see the beginning of an expansion of the hemline in the addition of flounces. Austen writes to Cassandra in 1813, "You really must get some flounces," and in the following year tells her friend Martha Lloyd, that dresses are "generally, though not always, flounced" (Le Faye 1997: 237, 273). Austen may have revised *Northanger Abbey* around 1816 (it was not published until after her death), but she didn't add any flounces to Catherine's dresses.

In Rolinda Sharples' painting some of the older women are wearing darker muslins—notably the plump lady in sprigged gray muslin in the foreground—but it is the light colored dresses that draw the eye. Eleanor Tilney, a model of good taste and elegance—and, as we have seen, encouraged by her brother—always wears white. Austen in her letters frequently refers to the prettiness and suitability of white. In 1801 she writes of a certain Mrs and Miss Holder who are generally judged to be detestable, but "their gowns are so white and so nice … that I cannot utterly abhor them" (Le Faye 1997: 66). White, of course, can have a symbolic function as a sign of purity and innocence in the dress of children and young women, and this will be taken very far in later nineteenth-century dress-requirements for unmarried girls; something that Henry James, for example, makes frequent use of in his fiction.

Although Austen is no "symboliste," when Mrs Allen is asked by her husband what she thinks of young women driving together with young men in an open carriage, she answers, "[o]pen carriages are nasty things. A clean gown is not five minutes wear in them. You are splashed getting in and getting out." That is not the problem, her husband says; the problem is that it looks "odd." Catherine is mortified; "[W]hy did you not tell me so before? I am sure that if I had known it to be improper, I would not have gone with Mr Thorpe at all" (Austen 1995 [1798]: 93). What Catherine actually wants from Mrs Allen is not fashion but moral guidance as to the propriety of such an excursion with the pushy John Thorpe. Mistakes

Figure 1
Rolinda Sharples: The Cloakroom, Clifton Assembly Rooms, 1817.

in propriety—"stains" on the purity of a girl's reputation—are less reparable than mud on white muslin. Elizabeth Bennet's muddy dress in *Pride and Prejudice*, we might remember, meets with Darcy's approval not censure, because it is a sign of Elizabeth's good heart, evidence that she has tramped across wet fields to be with her sick sister. We see here how Mrs Allen's obsession with dress, though comic in its effect, could indeed promote the "general distress" of the work. Her prattle on dress is, as Tony Tanner says, perhaps harmless, "but it can involve an inversion of values" (Tanner 1986: 60). If Catherine were to be guided by Mrs Allen she would order her conduct according to its effect on her clothes rather than on her moral standing. An outing with John Thorpe would be doubly dangerous: Catherine's physical welfare would be threatened by his reckless driving, and her reputation put at risk by being seen in his dubious company; damage to her muslin would be regrettable but reparable.

Why then is Henry Tilney's interest in dress different from that of Mrs Allen? We might reply that Henry's conversation with Mrs Allen on muslin is firstly made out of kindness and good manners: Henry sees that dress is her sole concern and so he unselfishly tailors his conversation to her interests. He does not expand on the topic of dress with anyone else. Mrs Allen, however, for all her good-heartedness, is, as we have seen, insensitive to others and harps on dress inappropriately— even dangerously. Henry's interest is also in the practical aspects of

muslin, its price and practicality, not in the latest style or color. More importantly, perhaps, it is a signal to Catherine of his denial of the separation between male and female spheres. He knows about dress, he is interested in it, he helps and advises his motherless sister in these matters and is happy to extend his expertise to Catherine. We are assured at the end of the chapter that Tilney is a clergyman of respectable family—in case we thought he was in the cloth trade. But he is nevertheless strange for his time: Evelina, the eponymous heroine of Fanny Burney's novel of 1778, makes fun of the expertise of male shop assistants in London: "so finical! so affected! They seemed to understand every part of a woman's dress better than we do ourselves; they recommended caps and ribbands with an air of so much importance, that I wished to ask them how long they had left off wearing them" (Burney 1997 [1778]: 73). We have to look to the end of the nineteenth century for a similar denial of the female monopoly of an interest in dress, when Henry James declared that "we are all of us extravagant, superficial and luxurious together" (James 1984: 24). John Thorpe's leering and self-interested pursuit of Catherine, his "macho" boastfulness, is much closer to the norm. But Catherine is never in any doubt as to which of the two men she prefers.

Henry's sensible remarks on dress are not only contrasted with Mrs Allen's silly ones but also with those of Isabella Thorpe, John Thorpe's sister. Catherine, endearingly if unguardedly naïve, warms to Isabella's gushing

overtures of friendship. They share an interest in gothic novels, parties and clothes and arrange to spend time together. Catherine is awed by Isabella's ability to compare the fashions of Bath with those of London, and Isabella is happy to "rectify the opinions of her new friend in many articles of tasteful attire" (Austen 1995 [1798]: 30). They meet in Bath's Pump Rooms and Isabella immediately overwhelms Catherine with a torrent of inconsequential chatter, ending in a jumble of fashion and literature: "Do you know, I saw the prettiest hat you can imagine, in a shop window in Milsom Street just now—very like yours, only with cocquelicot ribbons instead of green: I quite longed for it. But my dearest Catherine, what have you been doing with yourself all morning? Have you gone on with Udolpho?" (Austen 1995 [1798]: 36). Miss Andrews, a "particular friend" of Isabella's knows all the Radcliffe novels; "you would be delighted with her. She is netting herself the sweetest cloak you can conceive. I think her beautiful as an angel, and I am so vexed with the men for not admiring her!"(Austen 1995 [1798]: 37).

If Henry has given courteous attention to the problems of muslin, Isabella's prattle leaps from novels, her hats, her friend, to Catherine, and then to cloaks and men, revealing that her concern for her friends (or for literature) is as profound as for her hats. Her reference to the hat's "cocquelicot ribbons" does also, incidentally, place the novel in the 1790s, rather than revised around 1816, as bonnets in 1816 were small, fairly modest affairs compared with the immense confections of the 1790s (Figure 2). Isabella's final comment on Miss Andrews is pure malice. Catherine is much too candid and impressionable to see this as yet; but when Isabella's engagement to Catherine's brother, James, proves to be as enduring as cocquelicot ribbons, Catherine may wish she had noticed these signs of a fickle heart before.

This contrast between Isabella's self-centered superficiality and Henry's polite seriousness appears

Figure 2
Hats and Caps, *The Lady's Monthly Museum,* vol. 3, 1807, London: Vernor & Hood.

to be counteracted by a little sermon that Austen reads us on the foolishness of taking clothes too seriously. Catherine, in bed and thinking of what she will wear to the cotillion ball the following evening, lies awake "ten minutes … debating between her spotted and tamboured muslin." "Dress," Austen writes "is at all times a frivolous distinction, and excessive solicitude about it often destroys its own aim. Catherine knew all this very well; her great aunt had read her a lecture on the subject only the Christmas before." She longs to buy a new gown, but this "would have been an error of judgement." The heart of man is unaffected "by what is costly and new" in a woman's attire, and indifferent to "the texture of their muslin." This sounds like Austen's own voice, but when she ends by saying that "not one of these grave reflections troubled the tranquillity of Catherine" (Austen 1995 [1798]: 67), we remember that Catherine fell asleep in ten minutes and therefore did not actually allow the business of muslin gowns or moral reflections about them, to trouble her overmuch. These "grave reflections" have been delivered by a great aunt, but we know that Henry Tilney did in fact give considerable attention to the quality of Catherine's muslin. We might conclude that Austen, in self-mocking aunt-mode, causes Catherine to fall asleep during her lecture, secure in the knowledge that, on the contrary, Henry does care about the way she looks.

Catherine's education and discrimination has advanced sufficiently to judge and reject the advances of the crudely bullying

John Thorpe, and she escapes his threats to her happiness when she leaves Bath to stay with the Tilneys at Northanger Abbey. But she thrills to the prospect of other imagined "Gothic" dangers among crumbling ruins and supernatural possibilities of a medieval Abbey, a fantasy that Henry teasingly encourages on the journey there. Catherine is a little crestfallen when Northanger turns out to be a light, airy house, the subject of a costly modernization scheme being undertaken by Henry's father, General Tilney. "Improvement" of land and property was very much a part of the ethos of the new consumer and leisure society, and generally met with Austen's approval: Darcy is a model "improving" landlord in *Pride and Prejudice*. But General Tilney's schemes are motivated by snobbery and ostentation, as is his desire that Henry should court Catherine, for he believes, mistakenly, that she is an heiress.

The kindness of the Allens has introduced Catherine to the delights of this new consumer culture, and, for the occasion, has provided her with several muslin frocks (Figure 3). If Mrs Allen is in most respects a fool, she is also generous and indulgent, and is as likely to have been as extravagant over Catherine's muslin dresses as she was with her own. Catherine has now more formal gowns in a fashionable fabric than she strictly needs—something that presumably impressed General Tilney when he first saw her—as the General himself has a good deal more chinaware than *he* needs. He draws Catherine's attention to his breakfast service,

bought two years before, which he then dismisses as "old," and owns he is contemplating the purchase of another. This—unexpectedly perhaps—makes Tilney a typical product of the Romantic period. The social historian, Stana Nedanic, has pointed out that while Romanticism was critical of brute commercialism, it also encouraged focus on the self "and the cultivation of unstated emotions." "A permanently unfocused dissatisfaction, a longing for some hard to define emotional fulfilment," transferred itself to a longing "for those material objects that could act as proxy for the emotions and thus make them real" (Nedanic 1999: 210). Earlier religious and moralistic associations of luxury with vice, or with the corruption of a wealthy elite, had been replaced by economic considerations— shopping was good for the national economy—furthermore, "[l]uxury objects denoted a refinement of taste and expressed civility" (Berg 1999: 66). There is of course a difference between Catherine innocently dropping off to sleep, dreaming of new dresses, and General Tilney's plans to secure Catherine's imagined fortune to further his social ambitions. Austen, as Alistair Duckworth points out, is "deeply aware of a threatened change from a stable society based on Christian principles to a society in which money, or the appearance of money, is all that counts" (Duckworth 1971: 83).

Catherine does not like General Tilney, and senses his children's unease with him. Stimulated by her reading and by the Abbey's

Figure 3
Day and Evening Muslin Dresses,
The Lady's Monthly Museum, vol. 12,
1804, London: Vernor & Hood.

gothic setting, her over-active, uneducated imagination translates her dislike into a belief that the General has murdered his wife. Trembling in delicious fear, she opens an old chest in her bedroom, only to find a neat white cotton counterpane instead of moldering bones; and, in a stormy midnight, by guttering candlelight, she extracts a roll of papers from a black cabinet. In morning light this turns out to be not a bundle of blood or tear-stained letters, but a collection of recent laundry lists featuring such sinister items as shirts, stockings and cravats. Washable white cotton prevails again. When Catherine shortly afterwards betrays her lurid view of his father to Henry, his response is to urge on her his image of the security, openness and sanity of contemporary English life, as a reproof and a rebuttal of her fantasies, and a final, humiliating enlightenment.

But, of course, this isn't her final enlightenment, and Catherine is right to dislike the General, though for the wrong reasons. It is not the late Mrs Tilney who is finally the victim of the General's brutality, but Catherine herself. She is after all the heroine of a gothic novel of a sort. Catherine is a transparently nice girl, who has obviously won the affections of both Tilney's children, but when it emerges that her "appearance" as heiress to the Allens' fortune is a mistaken speculation of John Thorpe's, passed on to the greedy General, her virtues go for nothing, and she is bundled unceremoniously out of the Abbey to find her own way home. No murder, rape or torture takes place, but she confronts an emotionally and psychologically devastating experience, nonetheless, and in practical terms, her return home is a risky journey for an unprotected female. Dr. Johnson felt that one of the purposes of novel-writing was to teach the young how to avoid the snares laid by "Treachery for Innocence." Mrs Radcliffe had filled Catherine's fairly empty mind with images

of quite the wrong "snares," but Henry was also wrong to conclude that no snares exist in modern, sensible, well-washed England. Catherine's final, educated judgment of the General's behavior is a personal one, free from melodramatic prototypes, and Henry's speedy journey across country to claim Catherine's hand and admit his father's wrongdoing is an acknowledgement of the insufficiency of his earlier sanitized view of English society.

Catherine, of course, marries Henry—one of Austen's most attractive heroes. Henry can be pompous and patronizing at times, especially when undertaking the esthetic education of Catherine, but, as we have seen, he unhesitatingly, in romantic hero fashion, "rescues" Catherine from the consequences of his father's ill-treatment and declares his love for her. Is he, as Catherine nearly said, "strange"? As Marilyn Butler points out, Austen uses commodities, and dress in particular, to establish not only social and income distinctions but also moral differences: "Mrs Allen" Butler says, "damns herself in the reader's eyes by using anything so trivial as lace and muslin as her yardstick of quality." Nevertheless, "it is the appearance of commodities and their sophisticated treatment, that is deeply interesting ... [e]veryone in Bath becomes involved in the display or reading of signs" (Butler 1995: xxv). Tony Tanner, however, has made the interesting point that Austen does not seem to see dress-signs as part of a strategy in flirtation or courtship: "The emphasis is on narcissism not on seduction" (Tanner 1986: 63).

Henry quickly notices Catherine's dress and comments on it, which may be a signal of his appreciation of her, but unlike both John Thorpe and his own father, he does not read into her appearance her likely financial expectations. His teasing conversations with Catherine are like those with his sister and advance their intimacy; but he is also trying to "read" whether Catherine is capable of going beyond the formulaic exchanges between the sexes, and, although he sees the extent of her ignorance (as she does herself), he also establishes that she has a lively and educable mind. He finds that she is natural, honest and funny and their conversation begins to sound, in fact, very much like Jane Austen talking to Cassandra.

Henry is happy to give considered and informed attention to muslin, even although this appears an eccentric—even indecorous—topic for a young man meeting a young woman for the first time. But he also demonstrates that, unlike John Thorpe, he is equally well-informed on the contemporary novel, on recent ideas about art, and that he would happily discuss politics at length with Catherine—if she wants to, which she does not. In short, he denies that there is some mysterious barrier between male and female concerns, and that a girl, if reasonably informed, is not capable of a sensible discussion on grown-up subjects, and that topics such as dresses or novels cannot be treated seriously as well as amusingly, if the occasion warrants. When Austen said she enjoyed nothing so much as choosing a sponge cake, she was both making fun of herself, and being perfectly truthful. There is a time and a season for taking sponge cakes—and muslin—seriously. Butler sees Henry as a "mysterious, almost allegorical figure, who stands for androgynous ideas, youthful play, the comic spirit, romance" (Butler 1995: xliii). She sees him, in fact as Austen's double, or perhaps as her brother—inventive, playful, sharing an intimacy in which it is understood that hats or novels can be enjoyably discussed without losing a sense of proportion. We should recall that if *Northanger Abbey* has much about muslin, it also contains Austen's famous defense of the novel as a serious art form.

Mrs Allen's and Isabella's obsession with clothes and headgear is not only boringly self-centered for others to listen to (although entertaining to read about), but indicates a lack of discernment—"a displacement of concern" (Tanner 1986: 60). When Mrs Allen hears of the General's brutality to Catherine, she deplores it in the same breath as she tells Catherine that she has had "that frightful great rent in my best Mechlin [a kind of lace] so charmingly mended" (Austen 1995 [1798]: 207). Commodities are not, however, wicked in themselves and to read sermons about them is also boring. We leave Catherine generously provided for, and, we can assume, about to embark on a round of shopping for herself and her new home. The discussion of muslin brought Catherine and Henry together; his "strange" unabashed interest in the topic was perhaps the very thing that

marked him out as the man to fall in love with. Being something of a pedant, he will educate her, but because they share that sense of the ridiculous that marked their first conversation, it will not be the pupil/teacher relationship, for example, that seems to threaten the future of Emma Woodehouse's relations with Mr Knightley, or the intellectual bullying we see fifty years later in Casaubon's treatment of his wife, Dorothea Brooke in George Eliot's *Middlemarch*.

Catherine will enjoy that rare privilege of having a husband who can choose dresses with her, as well as swap novels and discuss them. Girls may read novels without endangering their purity as young men may talk of muslin without offending decorum. Austen may have been sparing in her fictional descriptions of dress— as in conversation, these things can be overdone—but her interest in the topic persists. As Tanner says, dress in Jane Austen's novels "at once reveals and conceals" (Tanner 1986: 63). And we might recall that her last written words, in a letter to a friend, were to recommend the wife and sister of a Captain Clement, who are "all good humour and obligingness, and I hope (since the fashion allows it) with rather longer petticoats than last year" (Le Faye 1997: 343).

References

Austen, Jane. 1995 [1798]. *Northanger Abbey*, Harmondsworth: Penguin Books.

Austen, Jane. 2000 [1954]. *Love and Friendship*. London: The Women's Press.

Belloc, Hilaire. 1968 [1907]. *Selected Cautionary Verses*. Harmondsworth: Penguin Books.

Berg, Maxine. 1999. "New Commodities, Luxuries and their Consumers in Eighteenth Century England," in Maxine Berg, *Consumers and Luxury*. Manchester: Manchester University Press.

Burney, Fanny. 1997 [1778]. *Evelina*. Boston: Bedford/St. Martin's.

Butler, Marilyn. 1995. Introduction to *Northanger Abbey*. Harmondsworth: Penguin Books.

Byrde, Penelope. 1999. *Jane Austen Fashion*. Ludlow: Excellent Press.

Duckworth, Alistair. 1971. *The Improvement of the Estate*. Baltimore: Johns Hopkins University Press.

James, Henry. 1984. *Literary Criticism: American and English Writers*. New York: The Library of America.

Le Faye, Deirdre (ed.) 1997. *Jane Austen's Letters*. Oxford: Oxford University Press.

Nedanic, Stana. 1999. "Romanticism and the Urge to Consume," in Maxine Berg (ed.) *Consumers and Luxury*. Manchester: Manchester University Press,

Ribeiro, Aileen. 1995. *The Art of Dress: Fashion in England & France, 1750–1820*. New Haven; Yale University Press.

Rothstein, Natalie. 1987. *Barbara Johnson's Album of Fashion and Fabrics*. London: Thames and Hudson.

Tanner, Tony. 1986. *Jane Austen*. Houndmills: Macmillan Education.

Dialog
Introducing the New "Dialog" Section of the Journal

Dialog

Textile: The Journal of Cloth and Culture is introducing a new section entitled "Dialog." This exciting development is designed to encourage the submission of *shorter* papers and articles that reflect current issues and concerns around textile theory and practice. Its aims will be to disseminate ideas and information and to encourage debate. Has something you read in *Textile* stirred you? Or is there an issue or topic that you would like to air?

If so, now is the time to let us know. This new section will offer an opportunity to engage in the sorts of dialog that we all find stimulating and helpful.

Papers for this section don't need to be referenced, and should ideally be between 1,000 and 5,000 words. They can be fully illustrated, or just text. They are not peer reviewed, but inclusion will be subject to editorial decision.

If you'd like to make a submission please contact the editorial assistant, or editors, in the first instance, who can provide additional information and advice. The inclusion of this section in issues of the Journal depends on your contribution, so we look forward to hearing from you.

The Editors

Textile, Volume 4, Issue 2, pp. 198–199
Reprints available directly from the Publishers.
Photocopying permitted by licence only.
© 2006 Berg. Printed in the United Kingdom.

Dialog
On the Outside, Looking In: The Iconography of the Outsider in Contemporary Fashion

Dialog
On the Outside, Looking In: The Iconography of the Outsider in Contemporary Fashion

I am on Coldharbour Lane in South London's Brixton, the original "front line," which, in 1984, was the location of full-scale urban riots. Although the area has long since been gentrified with smart bars and restaurants, the urban tension can still be felt beneath the polished exterior. Police tend to move in pairs and often look fearful, uncomfortable, excluded. Although the riots are a distant memory, drug dealing, muggings, traffic offences and verbal or physical assaults are not uncommon.

However, step into an independent fashion store called "Joy" on Coldharbour Lane and you will be effortlessly transported away from any edginess or negative feeling. In this enclosed world of baubles and kitsch, every item has been selected to bring a smile, joy, no less, to customers' faces. And I do find myself smiling, at a khaki, short-sleeved, button-down, men's summer shirt. Made from 100% cotton drill, it has a front breast pocket on the left-hand side. Above the pocket in black lettering are the initials and words "NYC Taxi." This is underscored by a strip of yellow chequered pattern (just like a New York taxi cab). Beneath this, the name TRAVIS BICKLE.

On the back of the shirt, in the lower right-hand corner is a sizeable black screen print (about the size of a man's outstretched hand). The image appropriated to decorate this shirt is from the film "Taxi Driver" (Martin Scorcese, 1976). It depicts Robert de Niro as the character Travis Bickle, head shaved into a mohican, staring away from the viewer and pointing two fingers at his own head. Colliding with this image at a 45-degree angle are the unpunctuated words, recalled—although not accurately—from the script of "Taxi Driver," delivered in a forbidding, black, gothic typeface: "One day a real rain will come and wash all the scum off the streets." On the same gradient but towards the bottom of the image and in a larger gothic font size is the character's name again, Bickle T.

The shirt, by a Belfast-based streetwear label called Apache

NILGIN YUSUF

Nilgin Yusuf is a Principal Lecturer in Fashion Journalism at The London College of Fashion

Textile, Volume 4, Issue 2, pp. 200–207
Reprints available directly from the Publishers.
Photocopying permitted by licence only.

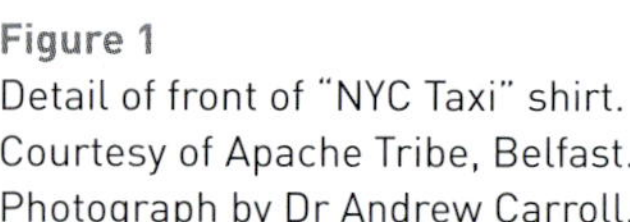

Figure 1
Detail of front of "NYC Taxi" shirt.
Courtesy of Apache Tribe, Belfast.
Photograph by Dr Andrew Carroll.

Tribe, is a basic item not notable for its design, cut, fabric, proportion or color. It is a standard men's shirt, mass produced and almost regulation in style. What makes it an item that draws the viewer in is the choice of screen print, words and images—the cultural referencing. Although the loose quote is something the narrator says at the beginning of the film, and the image is one from a scene of bloody carnage towards the end, they are reorganized and reinterpreted in a bold, post-modern way for maximum effect and drama. Celluloid reproduced onto cloth; a movie still for a moving body.

By way of its cultural referencing, the choice of words and images taken from the film will chime with anyone who has seen the movie and will, in turn, continue to chime with other "Taxi Driver" fans, a bit like wearing a particular football team's strip or scarf. It enables a select range of

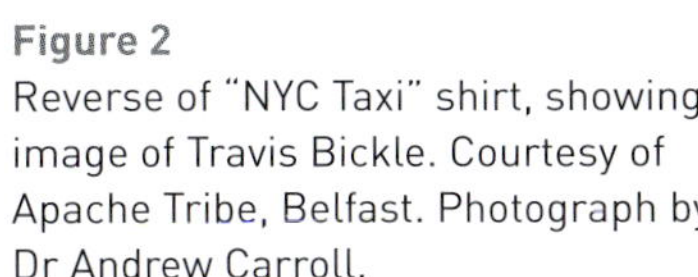

Figure 2
Reverse of "NYC Taxi" shirt, showing image of Travis Bickle. Courtesy of Apache Tribe, Belfast. Photograph by Dr Andrew Carroll.

consumers to join what Matt Hills describes in his exploration of Fan Cultures as a "community of the imagination" (Hills 2002: 180) On another level, by way of its playful monogramming, Apache Tribe has transposed the film's protagonist into the fabric of the actual garment. This enables the wearer of the shirt to pass themselves off as the aforementioned taxi driver, in a fun, lighthearted way.

Within the Apache Tribe collection, we can see that the use of monogramming is a recurring decorative device, allowing the wearer to indulge in humorous role play and assume an iconic identity. Their design "All Work and No Play Made Jack A Dull Boy" is another men's shirt, which echoes the Travis Bickle design but, instead, pays homage to Stanley Kubrick's film "The Shining" (1980)—another cinematic exploration of alienation. Instead of Robert de Niro, we have Jack Nicholson depicted at his most

crazed on the back of the shirt. Aside from the obvious attempts at dark humor, there is an interesting cultural element at work here. As observed by Roger Silverstone: "Within play, realities are suspended in favour of fantasies, since the rules of play are not those of ordinary, everyday life...it is in play that the game comes alive and gains uniqueness and significance" (Silverstone 1994: 169).

This exploration of self and social boundaries through role play and dressing up could equally be applied to the man himself, Travis Bickle, who in "Taxi Driver," spurned by the object of his amour, checks out of reality to pursue his dangerous fantasies. Initially, the Travis Bickle character is presented as a regular guy in a check shirt and jeans, an ex-marine of the Vietnam War, whose only faults appear to be working too hard and insomnia. His gradual descent into murderous fantasy sees him initially role playing, dressed up in

army fatigues with his head shorn, posturing endlessly in front of the mirror. Toting an entire arsenal of weaponry, he practices the lines of his newly defiant persona: "Ya talkin' to me?"

Although the words appear to be based on a recollection of the film—the actual quote is "Some day a real rain will come and wipe this scum off the streets" (or else the designers are cannily avoiding a copyright pitfall)—the combination of Travis Bickle's face and his disturbing philosophy give a sense of sound and vision; words inspired by the film, giving a voice to a two-dimensional representation. Without these elements, the garment would be unmemorable, anonymous. Without the film and the viewer's or wearer's response to the film, this item of clothing would have little or no interest whatsoever. As Baudrillard notes in *The System of Objects*: "What is consumed is never the object but the relationship signified, yet absent, simultaneously included and excluded. It is the idea of the relationship that is consumed in the series of objects that display it" (Baudrillard 1996: 201).

Back to the shirt in Coldharbour Lane, Brixton, and it is starting to strike me as a little weird that anyone would want to walk around wearing the image of a well-known psychopath, even a fictional one, on their back. After all, out there are potentially several real-life Travis Bickles wandering around, unhappy with their life and lot. Out there are all the social factors that invariably accompany the presence of crime in a densely populated inner-city area: fragmented social and community structures, lack of opportunity and poverty of the imagination. None of this is remotely amusing but, in here, the idea of "cool crime" has been recontextualized and repackaged, a covetable consumable object.

"Bickle is Elvis with a gun, doubled and multiplied. He is the cowboy John Wayne, the martyr James Dean, the rebel Brando. He is every American hero run amok, and the most ironic image of America since Jasper Johns painted the American flag." So wrote Jerry Saltz, art critic of *The Village Voice* in 1999, when critiquing the work of Douglas Gordon, a video artist who manipulates snips from iconic films—"Taxi Driver" being one. In 2001, celebrity footballer and men's fashion plate David Beckham was seen flaunting a Travis Bickle-inspired mohican. He confessed he had never seen the movie, but we can be pretty sure his hairdresser had. The

successful Scottish rock band Travis are named in homage to the man, while he has also featured in songs by The Clash and The Beastie Boys. There is now a Travis Bickle computer game on the market, where the player can assume the role of Travis Bickle, and the character even has his own website called "God's Loneliest Man." In 2004, readers of *Total Film* magazine voted him their favorite anti-hero.

So exactly who would wear this shirt? Clean, pristine, fresh smelling and empty? A genuine shirt of a bona fide taxi driver would be crumpled and creased, possibly stained with perspiration and the remains of food eaten on the hoof. The likelihood is that the Apache Tribe shirt will attact a college boy or university type, seeking to visibly boost his subcultural capital among his peer group. ("Hey, cool shirt.") I imagine this consumer, who can splash out the not inexpensive sum of £48 on a "fun" item, will not be driving a taxi or mini cab through the night. He will be studying for his next exams or saving for a downpayment on his first home. He will be saying, through his choice of clothing: look how knowing I am, how ironic and edgy. His choice of outsider chic, he hopes, will mark him out from the crowd.

Intellectuals and artists have a special predilection for the most risky but also the most profitable strategies of distinction, those which consist in asserting the power, which is peculiarly theirs, to constitute insignificant objects as works of art or, more subtly to give aesthetic redefinition to objects already defined as art, but in another mode, by other classes or class factions. (Bourdieu 1984: 283)

wrote Pierre Bourdieu in *Distinctions*. And indeed, while the populist appetite for crime literature, drama, films and limited-edition magazines continues unabated, there is a definite difference between these and the taste of the style afficionado who is tuned into the "aesthetics" or glamour of crime.

This enables the bourgeoisie to increase their highly developed cultural capital by "liking the same things differently, liking different things, less obviously marked out for admiration" (Bordieu 1984: 282).

One may ask why hip, urban culture is so keen to identify with the outsider. Travis Bickle, the name and the image, have become a kind of cinematic shorthand for dangerous psychopath but, by some kink in contemporary culture, this character has also become the epitome of cool, a cultish name to reference in conversation. From fashion to music, art, graphics and film, the influence of Travis Bickle has been reflected in myriad ways. Alain de Botton recently observed in *The Guardian*: "there are no more tempting targets for romantic fantasies than those misunderstood by others" (Botton 2005). And who could be more misunderstood than Travis Bickle? The archetypal outsider, a deviant and dangerous transgressive. He is the small man who seizes control and wreaks vengeance on the world. He is the invisible man

who suddenly finds a look, a role, a voice, and a purpose.

In the past, angry young types influenced by their filmic heroes may have donned a black leather jacket in deference to Marlon Brando in "The Wild One" or James Dean in "Rebel Without A Cause." But there is no such subtlety in this item of clothing, which loudly proclaims the object of its admiration. The attraction of outsiders has a long and noted history. Jean Genet's novel *The Thief's Journal*, a deeply romantic account of thieves, beggars, prostitutes and homosexuals, is a key text, which perhaps set the ball rolling for the wave of criminal chic in the late 1960s and early 1970s, from "Bonny & Clyde" to David Bailey's depiction of the Krays in his "Box of Pin Ups."

When discussing the creation of the Mods and Rockers, Stanley Cohen felt that "In the gallery of types that society erects to show its members which roles should be avoided and which should be emulated, these groups have occupied a constant position as folk devils: visible reminders of what we should not be" (Cohen 1973: 13). Conversely, this shows why to identify with "a type to be avoided" is so daring, so wild, so rock and roll. For a wearer to associate themselves with an outsider through dress is akin to buying all the brand values of outsider status: liberation, individuality, nonconformity. The outsider is the embodiment of personal freedom; unconditioned, free from social constraints and treading his own path.

With his essay *The White Negro* in 1967 Norman Mailer set the agenda for the aspirational outsider when he urged readers to "encourage the psychopath within," declaring "One is Hip or One is Square, one is a rebel or one conforms" (Mailer 1959: 89). Written in an era of rock and roll, beat poetry and emerging youth cultures, this challenge retains its forcefulness. "The superficialities of fashion may change, but the deep structure of cool as rebellious nonconformity provides us with a surprisingly stable and enduring set of guidelines. Cool, it seems has become, a social institution," note Heath and Potter in *The Rebel Sell* (Heath and Potter 2005: 198). If you log onto the Apache Tribe website (www.apache-tribe.com) you can read a little about the label's philosophy: "Apache Tribe is a lifestyle, not just threads. It's about setting out to cross lines and batter boundaries."

When something can be encapsulated so neatly, so easily formulated and formatted, so effortless to reproduce, it can be bought and sold, produced and consumed. Travis Bickle, the consummate outsider, becomes a textile print, heat transferred and multiplied, waiting to be hung in wardrobes and flaunted at fashionable parties. The wearer, of course, will bypass all the anxiety, neurosis, panic attacks, paranoia and disconnected, disembodied emotions and experiences of the genuine outsider. Instead, he will slip into this sanitized skin, bubble wrapped and vacuum packed, accepted by all of culturally aware society who have seen the movie "Taxi Driver" as witty and ironic.

"It's no more than a stance, a pose, an act of romantic sympathy" that provides a "passport into the nightmare world of the urban hipster, but his credentials remain forged, his journey into that world, illusionary, it's participation in that world, vicarious" wrote Dick Hebdige of Norman Mailer's *White Negro* (Hebdige 1974: 4).

It is fascinating that, thirty years after his creation, Travis Bickle, a fictional character invented by Paul Schrader (who wrote "Taxi Driver"), should have such a cult following, should still be so alive and potent a character for certain consumers today. The use of this archetypal outsider displayed so prominently on the shirt by Apache Tribe self-consciously plays to notions of hip culture. It uses the viewer's associations and references to lend drama and excitement to an otherwise mundane garment and has the potential to mark the wearer out as a rebel without them having to work for, or earn it.

On the Apache Tribe website we are informed that Mark E. Smith of rock band The Fall is a fan, as is Simon Pegg from "Spaced" and "Shaun of the Dead." This body of information is no doubt a reassuring one for the Apache Tribe fan, who can rest easy in his Travis Bickle shirt, knowing he is in good company, sharing threads and battering boundaries with other like-minded folk. Ultimately, it's a shirt that presents the iconography of the outsider, but is aimed at those comfortable individuals, doomed to live on the inside.

References

Baudrillard, Jean. 1996. *The System of Objects*. London: Verso.

Bourdieu, P. 1984. *Distinction: A Social Critique of the Judgement of Taste*. London: Routledge.

Botton, Alain de. 2005. *The Guardian Magazine*, July 2.

Cohen, Stanley. 1973. *Folk Devils and Moral Panics, The Creation of Mods & Rockers*, 3rd edn. London; Routledge.

Heath, Joseph and Potter, Andrew. 2005. *The Rebel Sell, How Counter Culture Became Consumer Culture*. Chichester: Capstone.

Hebdige, Dick. 1974. *The Kray Twins: A Study of a System of Closure*. Birmingham: University of Birmingham.

Hills, Matt. 2002. *Fan Cultures*. London: Routledge.

Mailer, Norman. 1959. *Advertisements For Myself*. New York: Putman.

Saltz, Jerry. 1999. *The Village Voice*, March 24–30.

Silverstone, Roger Silverstone. 1994. *Television & Everyday Life*. London: Routledge.

Exhibition Review
Lucy Orta, "Art for our time"

Exhibition Review

**Lucy Orta, "Art for our time"
The Curve, Barbican Art Gallery, London, September 15 to October 30, 2005**

Walking from Moorgate tube station I follow the yellow lines indicating efficient passage through the byways of the Barbican to its cultural center, an urban nomad, in a super-modern environment. Concrete-hard, pedestrian transit lanes intersect with each other, low level lighting floods the floor emphasizing the passage of anonymous feet through space. Surveillance cameras police and vet the travelers. No tented communities of displaced asylum seekers fill the gardens, no homeless sleeping-bagged forms curl up on the sofas of the public foyer, "it can be entered only by the innocent" Auge (1995: 102). It is for these "others" to inhabit the spaces of the margins, confined to detention centers, homeless shelters, roads, doorways and underpasses, hidden in shadows and out of sight. It is precisely these regions which concern Lucy Orta. In reviewing this exhibition I am reminded of the haunting words of Paul Virilio (1996): "For those about whom Lucy Orta speaks, today's street is hell."

The inspiration for Lucy Orta's work is the plight of millions of people globally, forced to the margins of society, made homeless by war, economic distress, political persecution and natural disaster. A world of people marginalized and rendered invisible by the indifference of the center. If seen at all it is through the comfortable detachment of television screens, heard only through soundbites, vilified and glorified in turn, all but forgotten by the time the red light on the television has dimmed. Her work speaks of a world in which the individual is increasingly deified and yet precariously isolated as societies continue to fragment. In response, it is concerned with examining the bonds that link individuals and communities and those that link the individual to their environment and the urban environment in particular. Its esthetic conjures up both an atmosphere of impending disaster and at the same time a staging of strong social bonds. Lucy Orta's work spans the boundaries of art, fashion, architecture and performance. Orta places the social ills of the world under scrutiny and, with an uncanny eye on her audience, her vision can be as disturbing as it is sensitizing.

Entering one end of the Curve Gallery in London's Barbican

REVIEWED BY DIANA DRUMMOND
Diana Drummond is Acting Critical Studies Coordinator for BA Textiles at Goldsmiths College, University of London.

Textile, Volume 4, Issue 2, pp. 208–213
Reprints available directly from the Publishers.
Photocopying permitted by licence only.
© 2006 Berg. Printed in the United Kingdom.

Centre, the viewer is confronted by *Urban Life Guards #0317* (2005), an army of faceless, but not voiceless, stretcher-bearers. The installation is an unnerving piece. It operates somewhere between fear and proposition, paranoia and practicality. "Are we ready for the worst?" reads the text screen-printed on their bodysuits. The uniform and uniformed, silver suited stretcher-bearers speak of a future already upon us. The silver bodysuits, hooded and reflective, deflect surveillance and yet have an authoritative presence. They unify the group into a harmonious and futuristic whole, highly visible, but at the same time anonymous and impersonal. In their grid formation they are at once formidable, purposeful and reassuring. They are the bearers of water, food and medicines, essential to survival. Their hi-tech silver, aluminum-coated, polyamide suits speak of the technologies at our disposal, available to NASA and the military and yet so infrequently brought to the aid of forced migrants in regions of natural or social disaster.

Lucy Orta's bodysuits speak of the potential of these resources and so appear as question marks writ large, as nightly we watched the plight of people stranded in the wake of hurricanes Katrina and Rita. Military resources are used to dislocate, de-territorialize, "keep order," but not to facilitate the survival of wrecked communities. Later they resurfaced as memories, as the European news media told its audience of the "inescapable" future suffering and loss of life that winter would bring to the homeless of the Pakistan/Indian earthquake. (It is worth noting here it was originally the plight of Kurdish refugees and the conflict in Rwanda that was critical to the inspiration of Orta's earlier *Refuge Wear* clothing.)

As I adjust to the environment of the Curve, I become aware of voices singing in unison, rising and falling; it is the deeply soulful, joyful cadence of the women of the Usindiso Women's Shelter, Johannesburg singing "God Bless Africa." An anthem and a protest song, their voices permeate the gallery and surround the viewer; from where do they come? From around, from above they begin to inhabit the bodysuits of the *Urban Life Guards*. They now move together to the human rhythm of song, bound together by culture, shared experience and a common humanity. No longer faceless, the bodysuits become approachable and the viewer becomes aware of text and printed talismans—compasses to re-orient the disoriented, ropes to reconnect peoples cast adrift, alienated and exiled, both symbolic of "Re Constructing"[1] networks and the interdependence of all human beings, one to the other. Like climbers bound together, clinging to the face of the mountain, or the survivors on the rooftops of New Orleans in the aftermath of Katrina, the urban citizen must reconnect centers to the margins, to reconfigure the relationship of citizens to each other and hence to the urban environment itself, before it and us are all laid to waste.

In *Urban Life Guards* each suit is equipped with ties and buckles for

Figure 1

N.U.O.≠0317, © Lucy Orta, artist. Lucy Orta holds the first Rootstein Hopkins Chair at London College of Fashion for the University of the Arts London. Twenty-three Military Stretcher beds, aluminum coated polyamide, surplus linen, silkscreen print, webbing, clips. Installation approx. 6 m × 25 m. Barbican Art Gallery, The Curve, 2005.

Figure 2

N.U.O.≠0317, © Lucy Orta, artist. Lucy Orta holds the first Rootstein Hopkins Chair at London College of Fashion for the University of the Arts London. Twenty-three Military Stretcher beds, aluminum coated polyamide, surplus linen, silkscreen print, webbing, clips. Installation approx. 6 m × 25 m. Barbican Art Gallery, The Curve, 2005.

connecting the stretcher-bearers one to another. The stretchers at waist height mirror the umbilical connections of Orta's *Nexus Architecture*, through which "the physical link weaves the social link" (Virilio 1996). Arranged uniformly in a grid, each unit can break away, emerge from the woven grid and engage in what Michel de Certeau (1984) described as the "art of doing." The creative process of everyday behavior, in the case of the *Urban Life Guard*, the assistance and care of fellow citizens in distress, a return perhaps to notions of the good Samaritan who chooses not to avert his eyes and walk on by, but to stop and lend assistance. I am reminded of the number of times I render invisible the homeless person at my feet as I remove cash from the cash machine, choosing instead to give my full attention to the disembodied instructions of the automated bank teller. I walk away reassured I can still withdraw £150 today. I will not allow my comfort to be interrupted by the plight of others. Yet Orta reminds us, "True peace is not only an absence of armed violence but a truly passive existence" (St. Augustine).[2]

Uniformity and repetition continue as a complex and multi-dimensional motif throughout the exhibition. They confront the audience with the dilemma of the relationship between the individual and society and between ideas of conformity and non-conformity. The uniformity of the suits not only reference a shared identity and social bonds, but also the loss of identity suffered by the marginalized in our society. We are reminded of the increasingly illusory nature of the individual as we submit ever more passively to Foucault's panopticism (Foucault 1995), and the monitoring, control and discipline of our movements and behavior. In examining the multiple readings of Orta's futuristic, repetitive and often uniform esthetic, the spectator is unwittingly trapped in the social and cultural conundrums confronting today's urban dweller. As bodysuits become shelters in *Body Architecture—Foyer D* (2002), the portable environment offers protection and collaboration, but also represents the confinement of living on the margins. Ideas of physical and behavioral, coerced and self-imposed disciplines and restrictions are explored in the exchanges between passers-by and the testimonies of prisoners held at the Maison d'Arrêt de Metz in Orta's *Commune Communicate* (1996) project.

The exhibition presents an examination of the value systems on which we accept and reject, associate, consume and discard, and between the pure and the defiled. Orta's *All in One Basket—Les Halles* (1997) and *Hortirecycling Enterprise* (1999) do more than simply confront the appalling and callous waste of food and resources in Western consumer practice, but provide a metaphor for society as a whole. They highlight the designation of value in consumer culture, through surface and packaging. We are persuaded through cinema, television and advertising of the need to strive for the idealized body—be that body a piece of fruit, a bottle of perfume, our own body or the body of another. We have learnt to distinguish between the pure and the defiled on the basis of perfection and place. We search for our fruit and vegetables on the supermarket/market shelves, turning each over for inspection, rejecting any "abnormality," selecting only those that appear smooth, unblemished, perfectly formed, with no trace of the earth. All that has fallen, been misplaced, is soiled, irregular or rough, we reject for fear of the unknown or lest we too become contaminated by association. We pick up off the street at our own peril and at the cost of our reputations. Scavenger I am not.

What is striking in Lucy Orta's work is its ambition. It challenges, confronts, examines and engages on local and global scales; staged as often on the street as in the art gallery, the work advocates social intervention and is both performance and social activism. It is easy to be reminded of Modernist agendas seeking to break down the barriers that compartmentalize society and interventions to create a new social conscience. *Refuge Wear Intervention London East End* (1998) places Orta's architectonic, transformable clothing in front of a Modernist block for social

housing in London's East End. It is an effective juxtaposition; the rational, abstract, geometric ordering of the Modernist block is counterpoised by the organic and gestural architecture of the body proposed by Orta. Her work results not from a Modernist, pedagogical approach, but from collaborations and discourse with diverse social groups locally and internationally. This is given physical expression in *70 × 7 The Meal*, Act XXIII of which was staged at the Curve as part of the exhibition. *The Meal* has traveled all over Europe and as far afield as the Napa Valley, USA, and Mexico City. Over the ritual of the meal, diners engage in a discourse on production, resources, distribution and access to the raw materials of the meal.

Just as the Brutalist architecture of the Barbican responds daily, seasonally and annually to both culture and nature, to the seasons, the weather and the skies of the urban environment, so Orta's modular architecture is adaptable to sites, personalities and communities. It is responsive to the gestures of the body, the patterns of diverse cultures and the needs of various climates and topographies. Orta advocates a renewed "Respect"[3] for the power of collective activity and

solidarity, to confront a world in which humanity is all too easily reduced to an organized system of efficient packaging, a world where identities and beliefs are transformed into corporate logos and uniformly stenciled, neatly, onto our clothing and our bodies, stratifying and sorting the good from the bad, the innocent from the guilty, the worthy from the disposable.

Notes

1. Text screen-printed on bodysuits of *Urban Life Guards #0317*.
2. Ibid.
3. Ibid.

References

Auge, Marc. 1995. *Non-Places: An Introduction to an Anthropology of Supermodernity*. London/New York: Verso.

de Certeau, Michel. 1984. *The Practice of Everyday Life*. Berkeley: University of California Press

Foucault, Michel. 1995. *Discipline & Punish: The Birth of the Prison*. New York: Vintage Books.

Virilio, Paul. "Urban Armour." Cited in Orta, Lucy. 1996. *Refuge Wear*. Paris: Editions Jean-Michel Place, p. 3/6.

Book Reviews

Book Review

Pacific Pattern, Susanne Küchler and Graeme Were; Photography by Glenn Jowitt (London: Thames and Hudson, 2005)

Through stunning photographs and well-researched texts, anthropologists Susanne Küchler and Graeme Were, together with photographer Glenn Jowitt demonstrate that patterns in the Pacific are not just beautiful; they also play an important role in architectural structures and fabrics, thus carrying ideas fundamental to Pacific societies. Similarities between Pacific island cultures and case studies from Polynesian and Melanesian cultures are considered. *Pacific Pattern* guides the reader through the most important themes in Pacific material cultures while acquainting them with its scholars.

The introductory chapter highlights the importance of patterns and presents a journey through several periods of Pacific history: Asian peoples, plants and animals populated mainland New Guinea some 40 000 to 50 000 years ago; technological advances led to agriculture, animal husbandry, pottery, barkcloth and the outrigger canoe around 5000 years ago; the colonization of Eastern Polynesia happened 1500 years later; finally the first Europeans arrived in the sixteenth century. The introduction concludes with "Plants and their Uses: Coconut, Pandanus and Barkcloth," a slightly misleading title as the section mainly concerns wooden objects. Moreover, "barkcloth," strictly speaking, is a paper mulberry tree product, and not a plant. That said, the discussion of the indigenous plants, coconut, pandanus and paper mulberry tree is accurate and informative.

In Chapter One, "A History of Pattern in Fibre and Fabric in the South Pacific," the authors touch on the issues of European exploration and the stereotypes Europeans attributed to the peoples encountered. Collecting flourished in the nineteenth century. It brought about the founding of ethnographic museums and the idea to treat artifacts as scientific specimens. Christianity, established by missionaries of different denominations, had a profound influence on materials and techniques: the introduction of European-style dress prompted the Pacific people to adapt their traditional materials such as barkcloth or to switch to sewing and crochet techniques. Most of the Pacific was colonized by the major nineteenth- and twentieth-century powers. For example, New Guinea was divided between

Textile, Volume 4, Issue 2, pp. 214–217
Reprints available directly from the Publishers.
Photocopying permitted by licence only.
© 2006 Berg. Printed in the United Kingdom.

REVIEWED BY FANNY WONU VEYS

Germany, Great Britain and the Netherlands; the Austral Islands, the Marquesas, the Society Islands and New Caledonia still belong to France—the authors do not include the Western Polynesian islands of Uvea (Wallis) and Futuna as part of the French overseas territories; the Hawaiian islands were annexed and are now the fiftieth US state; Guam and American Samoa remain US territories, while the independent Caroline islands and Palau still maintain strong links with American administration. Attracted by economic opportunities many Pacific islanders moved to New Zealand, Australia and North America.

"Traditional Pattern: Techniques and Media" explores techniques and materials used in fiber-based objects including string, cordage, cloaks, capes, helmets, basketry, matting and barkcloth. New Zealand Maori cloaks exemplify the "sacred nature of the thread" in Polynesia while examples drawn from Micronesia, Samoa, Hawaii, Fiji and New Ireland demonstrate that utilitarian fiber-based objects visualize cultural concepts of time, space, rank, kinship and clan ties next to being ritually significant through their linking capacities.

The authors recount in "Contemporary Pattern: Materiality and Modernity" how cloth and European sewing techniques were adopted to suit nineteenth-century missionary body politics. Contemporary Pacific fashion displayed in New Zealand shows, Cook Islands sporting events and in churches expresses specific island and/or village identities which in urban centers are reflected and reinvigorated by the creation of baskets, hats, flower leis, decorative girdles and cushion covers with recycled materials such as plastic carrier bags, packaging tape and unraveled sweaters.

In "Pattern in Architecture and Interior Design" the authors explain that in Pacific society the house is not just a dwelling, but an essential harbor of the principle of life. For Melanesian societies the Papuan Gulf men's houses—buildings which serve as ritual spaces for initiated men—induce the living, growing and containment of life forces. In Polynesia the primary purpose of walls and thatches is to hinder and contain the flow of invisible forces. The study of Pacific church buildings reveals that the fiber pattern was and continues to be a fundamental part of their architecture, regulating the permeability of the enclosure.

The house—body link expressed in the similar patterns enveloping both is demonstrated in "Patterns on the Body." Through the attention paid to the patterns occurring on different types of sarong and upper-garments made of barkcloth, cloth and other fibers, the principle of layering is touched upon: several layers of patterns are superimposed, which in Polynesia is a way of creating several skins, thus redressing the problematic permeability of the body. Hair, painting, tattooing and scarification are discussed in separate sections. Both in Melanesia and Polynesia patterns are shared between a variety of body-covering media and other objects.

The final chapter, "Patterns of the Mind," containing two

extensively worked-out case studies based on fieldwork, examines how patterns transcend their materiality. Especially in the Pacific, where the population is dispersed over wide distances and with most of its islands' diaspora communities living in the urban centers of New Zealand, Australia and North America, pattern is found to bridge these spatial divides. In the section "String and Square in Tonga" the authors argue that Tonga had and has a fiber-based technology: barkcloth, woven aprons and crochet work reflect rank and status; moreover, numerous barkcloth designs are recorded in string-figure looping. "Layer and Lattice in the Cook Islands" reveals that in Eastern Polynesia, the techniques of sewing, cutting, superimposing layers of cloth replaced the making of barkcloth and mats, a practice lost with the coming of the missionaries who destroyed the clothed wooden sculptures. Today, *tivaivai* (quilts) of which there are three types in the Cook Islands— those composed of hundreds of diamond squares, the appliquéd quilts and the cut-out ones—reflect the preoccupation with coloring and superimposing of layers that existed in barkcloth and matting.

This book demonstrates that pattern in the Pacific is not only a physical matter: it captures temporal, spatial and cultural modes of setting oneself, thus intertwining mental and material conditions for life. The photographs and their captions illustrate the argument excellently.

Book Review

Silk and Empire, Brenda King (Manchester: Manchester University Press, 2005)

The history of Britain's relationship with India could be written as a series of studies of individuals like Sir Thomas Wardle, who lies at the center of this well-researched book. (Thomas Holbein Hendley was another from the same mold, with pioneering dual careers in eye surgery and museum curatorship in Jaipur—someone should write a book about him too...) Brenda King makes a valiant champion for Wardle, a remarkable man who taught William Morris dyeing and printing at his factory in Staffordshire but who remained basically a small-scale figure in the history of textile production in Britain. The story of Wardle's personal commitment to the improvement of the Indian silk industry makes engrossing reading. Starting with his father's experiments with dyeing the notoriously impervious *tasar* (wild) silk in Macclesfield, Wardle made the dyeing and block-printing of this rough type of silk his main focus. He was fascinated by dyes, and was one of the first to see the danger to India's indigenous dyeing skills posed by the new synthetic colors. His first visit to India in 1885–86 at the age of 54 saw him traversing the country on his rail pass visiting centers of silk production and coming to understand at first-hand the difficulties faced by Indian weavers, while at the same time appreciating their skills more and more. He returned to India in 1903, at the age of 72, in order to try to revive the Kashmiri silk industry. In this he had some success, albeit short-lived.

Wardle was equally committed to improving the English silk industry, through better standards of design and the inspiration of textiles such as Indian woven silks, which he (like many others of his time) considered supreme examples of textile design. He wrote and lectured extensively on the subject, and donated specimens to museums so that textile designers could come and study them. Amazingly, he also collected at his own expense for the Chamber of Commerce in Lyons—far from seeing the French silk-weavers as rivals, Wardle was exceptional in having a vision of collaboration that was in stark contrast to the cut-throat business minds of the day.

As well as bringing Wardle out of the shadow of his more illustrious contemporaries, King also sheds light on the little-known collections of Indian textiles

Textile, Volume 4, Issue 2, pp. 218–219
Reprints available directly from the Publishers.
Photocopying permitted by licence only.
© 2006 Berg. Printed in the United Kingdom.

REVIEWED BY ROSEMARY CRILL

that were assembled with the intention of inspiring design and manufacture in weaving centers such as Macclesfield. Pieces from these collections are illustrated, together with fascinating archive photographs that show the practical application of Indian techniques in England— for example, who knew that traditional Indian tie-dyeing was being carried out in Macclesfield, and as late as 1948?

This is all excellent material, and there is much that is new here. But there is a recurring feeling throughout the book that King has tried to shoe-horn this information into a broader academic argument that does not really stand up. While no-one would disagree that northern textile collections are under-explored, it seems odd to suggest that they are part of "a trading relationship long overlooked" between India and England (p. xix) when books on the subject fill many shelves. *Silk and Empire* may be a pleasingly catchy title, but it is a misleading one: rather than the broad sweep of history, trade and manufacture that it suggests, the book analyses a very specific time and place in the history of textile design in Britain in the late nineteenth century. The positive impact of Indian designs (on metalwork and architecture as well as textiles) on influential British opinion-formers like Owen Jones and William Morris has always been acknowledged—the Indian objects shown at the Great Exhibition in 1851, for example, were hugely influential—and yet the author claims more than once that her book somehow overturns negative "orientalist" preconceptions in this area. There are also mistakes in the rather sketchy (and I think unnecessary and often irrelevant) overview of Indian silk textiles (Chapter Three)—tie-dyeing and ikat are confused on p. 59, for example, and "atlas" is repeatedly described as a form of wild silk when it is in fact a satin-weave textile. There are other infelicities which should have been edited out— Chapter seven is entitled 'The Arts and Crafts Movement and Indian Silk', while it is headed on every page 'The Arts and Crafts Movement in India' which never existed.

These caveats apart, within this book lies a worthwhile study of one of textile history's less frequented corners. A tighter focus on the subject would have made it a more satisfying book to read and consult, as it is here that Brenda King has something new and interesting to say.

Book Reviews

Medieval Clothing and Textiles (Vol. 1), Robin Netherton and Gail R. Owen Crocker (eds) (Woodbridge: The Boydell Press, 2005)

Clothing Culture 1350–1650, Catherine Richardson (ed.) (Aldershot: Ashgate, 2004)

Medieval Clothing and Textiles is actually the first issue of a periodical. It comes out of a well-established network of scholars working on dress and textile history who lecture annually at the international medieval conferences at Kalamazoo, MI, USA and Leeds, UK. While a timescale for subsequent issues is not given, there is nevertheless the promise of more to come from a large existing repertoire and from potential new contributors. The first volume contains ten varied and interesting articles. The first three cover material from Anglo-Saxon England, the rest range broadly from articles on clerical dress, textile references in English wills and two on costume details: the tippet in English fourteenth-century dress and the veil worn by Giovanna Cenami in Jan Van Eyck's Arnolfini portrait. Of particular note are Elisabeth Coatsworth's important historical survey of Anglo-Saxon embroidery, which could easily lay the foundations for a more substantial study, and John Muendel's detailed analysis of the technology of medieval fulling mills. But the collection also includes more culturally oriented studies, such Maren Clegg Hyer's article on the Exeter Book, which considers the oblique and lateral uses of riddle and metaphor in textile imagery and Sandra Ballif Straubhaar's reconsideration of the conventions for color, especially blue, in the dress of Icelandic slayers.

Clothing Culture is an edited collection in Ashgate's series: "The History of Retailing and Consumption." Like *Medieval Clothing and Textiles*, it arose from conference papers, but in this instance, a single event held at the University of Kent, rather than a disparate collection over a long period. It therefore benefits as a book, from a greater degree of coherence and also from a thoughtful introduction by the editor, Catherine Richardson, laying out the underlying theory and rationale for approaches to costume and textile studies from more anthropological and culturally holistic standpoints. The fifteen articles by an group of scholars from around the (western)

REVIEWED BY VERONICA SEKULES

Textile, Volume 4, Issue 2, pp. 220–221
Reprints available directly from the Publishers.
Photocopying permitted by licence only.

world, ranging in experience from recent PhD graduates to senior academics like Elisabeth Hallam, Maria Hayward and Elisabeth Salter, are biased towards the later Middle Ages, and establish a really interesting and wide-ranging international landscape for costume and textile studies, taking the subject far into social, political, economic, textual and moral issues. It is organized under four headings, although there are overlaps between them: "Fabrics of Nation," with articles considering such issues as indigenous and imported costume and the use of dress to form or reinforce national identities. "Marking Distinctions" is especially concerned with social identities and nuances of interpretation of costume, or lack of it in terms of moral and philosophical debate. "Material Movements" (overlapping somewhat with "Fabrics of Nation") covers politics and international relations and "Discourse, Body and Gender," which could easily have within it many of the articles which appear in other sections, concentrates on dress as display and the culture of revealing and concealing the body.

Both these books establish, in their different ways, new standards for costume and textile historians, showing just some of the possibilities of interdisciplinary study. They exemplify the best of recent trends in textile and dress history to consider these subjects, which might always fall prey to superficial or overly technical treatment, within broad cultural, social and political contexts.

Book Review

Textiles of the Wiener Werkstätte, 1910–1932, 2nd edn, Angela Volker (London: Thames and Hudson, 2004)

The reissue of the 1994 publication explores printed and woven textiles produced by the Wiener Werkstätte now housed in the Austrian Museum of Applied Arts. Although general Wiener Werkstätte publications exist, Volker specifically documents the printed and woven textile collection, which has been neglected as a separate area. Her position as head of the textiles department for over 30 years has allowed her to study, in depth, the extensive range of material in the collection and her work cataloging it is reflected in this book.

The Wiener Werkstätte was founded by Josef Hoffman, Koloman Moser and Fritz Waerndorfer in 1903 and comprised a group of craftspeople whose skills were as diverse as the materials they used to produce handcrafted products. Volker follows the development of the fashion and textile department, which was founded around 1910. The book begins by describing the archive and its contents, which includes sample cards and books, designs, garments, fabrics, ribbons, lace, embroidery, printing blocks, photographs and press cuttings. Volker then goes on to discuss the system of archiving the material and methods of dating objects. She also discusses the location of items outside of the Museum's collection, which is useful for the specific study of Wiener Werkstätte textiles. The description of archiving and dating pieces, combined with the catalog at the back of the book, is especially useful for the study of individual artists or periods or the development of design within this particular company. It is also useful for curators and museum staff as a comparative system and as a definitive guide to identifying objects that might be in other collections. The catalog lists designs by artist, while the concordance lists designs by pattern name.

Volker then details the chrono-logical history of the textile depart-ment, changing and developing styles, methods of production, examples of use and consumption. Finally, a chapter is devoted to the most prestigious designers.

Glorious color photographs complement the text, reflecting the collection and often illustrating a production process. For example, three photographs might show a textile design on paper, the printed textile, and the textile made up into a garment.

REVIEWED BY SARAH MAGILL

Textile, Volume 4, Issue 2, pp. 222–223
Reprints available directly from the Publishers.
Photocopying permitted by licence only.
© 2006 Berg. Printed in the United Kingdom.

The book is a valuable source for designers and artists of all genres from textile to graphic design; abstract art to sculpture. It is also a helpful resource for economic, social and textile historians, to name a few, as the sections on production and distribution offer historical insight into production techniques and methods and rates of consumption of the products. For those who wish to specifically study the Wiener Werkstätte textiles collection of the Austrian Museum of Applied Arts, this book is the authoritative source.

Book Review

Textiles of the Arts and Crafts Movement, Linda Parry (London: Thames and Hudson, 2005)

The reissue of *Textiles of the Arts and Crafts Movement*, originally published in 1988, coincides with the Victoria and Albert (V&A) Museum's exhibition, *International Arts and Crafts*, which ran from March to July 2005. Linda Parry acted as curator on the V&A's William Morris exhibition in 1996 and was a consultant for the 2005 exhibition.

The book covers the years from 1888, when the Arts and Crafts Exhibition Society was founded and opened its first exhibition, to 1916, a point which marks a change in style and an exhibition at the Royal Academy, a body against which the artists were acting when they established the society. The introduction sets the scene for the book by exploring reasons behind the founding of the movement, in particular dissatisfaction towards the undemocratic nature of the Royal Academy and its selection committee. Parry then charts the members' artistic and industrial backgrounds from the mid-nineteenth century, the evolution of style and the contemporary fashions for home furnishings, before a chapter devoted to the textiles involved in exhibitions. These included embroideries, printed and woven textiles, both patterned repeats and individual motifs. This chapter is divided by date into three sections, 1888–1890, 1893–1903, and 1906–1916, which Parry feels reflects the technical and stylistic advances. The final chapter explores the designers, manufacturers and shops, and the book is capped off by a detailed and highly useful catalog of "designers, craftsmen, institutions and firms," which details names, dates, artistic leanings, associations with other designers and/or firms, exhibits, and general history.

The textiles discussed are mainly home-furnishing textiles and modes, such as wall panels and hangings, furnishing fabrics and carpets, rather than clothing and worn textiles. The book boasts 91 color illustrations, mainly of the textiles themselves, which are fabulous, taken especially for the publication, and often filling the entire page. There are also contemporary photographs, for instance, of room settings and the designers themselves. The bibliography has been updated for the new edition and includes books published after 1990. The primary sources are mainly the actual textiles held in the V&A,

REVIEWED BY SANDRA BROCKWELL

Textile, Volume 4, Issue 2, pp. 224–225
Reprints available directly from the Publishers.
Photocopying permitted by licence only.
© 2006 Berg. Printed in the United Kingdom.

with a small number of exhibition catalogues and reviews.

This book would be a worthwhile resource for those researching the Arts and Crafts movement as a whole, any one of the designers and artists involved, societies, firms and outlets. The large number of color plates allows the reader to see styles evolve, and illustrate points made in the text.

Book Review

Lace from the Victoria and Albert Museum, Clare Browne
(London: V&A Publications, 2004)

Clare Browne presents an incredible selection of laces as well as a brief, concise history of lace production and marketing. This history describes the influence of economics, technology, trade, politics and fashion on the making of lace and vice versa. Looking at the progress of a product over time is an enjoyable way of studying the past. The roles of individuals—lace designers and makers, royalty, financial ministers, inventors, consumers—and the display of wealth and position also are a significant part of the story.

Lace pictures 100 needle-and-bobbin laces with many close-up views. Those with colored components are in color. Amazingly, almost forty percent of the fabrics in the book date before 1700, so the earliest laces made are well represented. Browne has included only half as many eighteenth-century laces as those from the seventeenth and nineteenth centuries, which is surprising, but this distribution may represent the strengths of the collection, as delicate silk laces do not survive well.

The selections from many different geographic areas include furnishings fabrics, a few garments, and many accessories, but except for a cap, a sleeve flounce and purses, most are two-dimensional. The apparel items include aprons, caps, a chasuble, collars, cravats, fan leafs, a fichu, lappets, a parasol cover, sleeve ruffles, shawls, stoles and veils. In lieu of garments and accessories on mannequins, Browne includes five color portraits, although seeing one of the overdresses or skirts that she often mentions would have been enlightening.

The examples provide good contrast between the geometric designs of the earliest laces, the dense or heavy baroque-style laces, the lighter rococo-era fabrics, and the reinvented patterns of later times. Browne describes the influence of woven silk textiles on lace patterns and construction. She frequently discusses thread size, a major determinant in the appearance, stiffness and durability of the final product. The introduction often mentions chinoiserie, but the plates include no examples with typical chinoiserie figures, bridges or roofs, although at least four have blossoms and leaves that could be identified as having oriental characteristics. Plate 49

Textile, Volume 4, Issue 2, pp. 226–227
Reprints available directly from the Publishers.
Photocopying permitted by licence only.

REVIEWED BY MARGARET ORDOÑEZ

shows a figure that looks more Ottoman than Chinese.

The photography shows the lace details better than most lace books. Browne includes references to many plates in the introductory historic overview. She has a brief, up-to-date bibliography, but no index. This is disappointing, as the introduction contains much information, despite being only eleven and a half pages long. This omission is a hindrance to researchers and anyone who would like to use the book as a reference.

The book also lacks confirmation of fiber content, which could have been included in the descriptions. Indeed, I have become particularly interested in fiber content of laces since Angharad Rixon's (2002) discovery of cotton and flax blended in sixteenth and seventeenth-century lace yarns. Using polarized light at the University of Rhode Island, Mary Beth Gale and I also have found the same blending in many eighteenth-century printed fabrics (Gale 2001). With all the work that goes into the research and publication of a book like this, omitting an important part of the analysis diminishes the scholarly contribution of the book. Having this knowledge helps readers identify laces in their collections. Browne does include some fiber information, such as lace makers' outlining patterns with horsehair

(Plate 40), using non-shiny silk in some nineteenth-century black French laces, and making post-1850s Brussels laces of cotton. Similarly valuable are the inclusions about non-shiny silk in some nineteenth-century black French laces and post-1850s Brussels laces being made of cotton.

I particularly like the amazing needle lace in Plate 31, a very large seventeenth-century French furnishing flounce. The many motifs connected with bars contain various open patterns that add variety to the textile. One piece of a set, it is a needlework masterpiece. Likewise, the seventeenth-century all-lace Italian chasuble in Plate 22 is an extraordinary textile. On a more whimsical side, seventeenth-century stumpwork influenced the makers of three-dimensional English needle lace in Plate 42. Again, a wide variety of needlework stitches along with seed pearls and glass beads create many different patterns in this sophisticated version of stumpwork.

More seventeenth and eighteenth-century examples of metallic lace would have been good, but the selection of fabrics to include in the book must have been very difficult. A number of examples do, however, provide variety. A close-up view of the seventeenth-century silk-covered gimp and parchment lace in Plate

35 is an excellent example and would definitely help a researcher identify a similar lace. Likewise, the near view of a hollie point square in an eighteenth-century sampler in Plate 57 clearly shows how it differs from other types of needle laces.

Claire Browne's *Lace* provides many examples from the Victoria and Albert Museum's renowned lace collection that usually are not on public display. It has value as a reference book because of the close-up photographs and the introductory historic overview. In addition, the beauty of the pieces and their patterns offers pleasurable viewing as well as many sources of inspiration for artists. Browne's *Lace* is a valuable resource for any lover of lace and history.

References

Gale, Mary Beth. 2001. "Indigo-Resist Prints from Eighteenth-Century America: Production and Provenance." Master's thesis, University of Rhode Island.

Rixon, Angharad. 2002. "A Fault in the Thread? Examining Fibers Taken From Laces of the Sixteenth and Seventeenth Centuries." Strengthening the Bond: Science and Textiles, Preprints, North American Textile Conservation Conference, Winterthur, DE, 5–6 April, pp. 101–9.

CALL FOR PAPERS
2006 MRS FALL MEETING
www.mrs.org/fall2006/

**ABSTRACT DEADLINE:
JUNE 20, 2006**

In fairness to all potential authors, late abstracts will not be accepted.

Meeting Chairs:

Babu R. Chalamala
Indocel Technologies, Inc.
Tel   919-244-1040
Fax   888-853-4407
chalamala@indocel.net

Louis J. Terminello
Lawrence Livermore National
   Laboratory
Tel   925-423-7956
Fax   925-422-0029
terminello1@llnl.gov

Helena Van Swygenhoven
Paul Scherrer Institute
Tel   41-56-310-2931
Fax   41-56-310-3131
helena.vs@psi.ch

For additional meeting information,
visit the MRS Web site at

www.mrs.org/meetings/

or contact:

**Member Services
Materials Research Society**

506 Keystone Drive
Warrendale, PA 15086-7573
Tel 724-779-3003
Fax 724-779-8313
E-mail: info@mrs.org
www.mrs.org

SYMPOSIA

SOFT MATTER—ACTIVE MATERIALS, HYBRIDS, AND SENSORS

A: Responsive Soft Matter—Chemistry and Physics for Assemblages, Films, and Forms
B: Structure, Processing, and Properties of Polymer Nanofibers for Emerging Technologies
C: Smart Dielectric Polymer Properties, Characterization, and Their Devices
D: Biosurfaces and Biointerfaces
E: Nanofunctional Materials, Nanostructures, and Novel Devices for Biological and Chemical Detection
F: Integrated Nanosensors
G: Fibrillar Aggregates as Materials—Assembly, Properties, and Applications
H: Biofilm-Material Interactions—New Tools, Technologies, and Opportunities

ELECTRONICS, PHOTONICS, AND MAGNETICS

I: Advances in III-V Nitride Semiconductor Materials and Devices
J: Diamond Electronics—Fundamentals to Applications
K: Zinc Oxide and Related Materials
L: Group IV Semiconductor Nanostructures
M: Quantum Dots—Growth, Behavior, and Applications
N: Self Assembly of Nanostructures Aided by Ion- or Photon-Beam Irradiation—Fundamentals and Applications
O: Nanostructured and Patterned Materials for Information Storage
P: Nanoscale Magnets—Synthesis, Self-Assembly, Properties, and Applications
Q: Nanowires and Carbon Nanotubes—Science and Applications
R: Meta-Materials at the Milli-, Micro-, and Nanoscale
S: Organic Electronics—Materials, Devices, and Applications
T: Ferroelectrics and Multiferroics
U: Advances in *In Situ* Characterization of Film Growth and Interface Processes

V: Advanced Electronic Packaging
W: Heterogeneous Integration of Materials for Passive Components and Smart Systems
Y: Enabling Technologies for 3-D Integration

ENERGY STORAGE AND UTILIZATION

Z: Hydrogen Storage Technologies
AA: Solid-State Ionics
BB: Mobile Energy
CC: Solar Energy Conversion

MICROSTRUCTURE, MECHANICS, AND MODELING

DD: Mechanics of Biological and Bio-Inspired Materials
EE: Size Effects in the Deformation of Materials— Experiments and Modeling
FF: Processing-Structure-Mechanical Property Relations in Composite Materials
GG: Multiscale Modeling of Materials
HH: Thermodynamics and Kinetics of Phase Transformations in Inorganic Materials
II: Advanced Intermetallic-Based Alloys
JJ: Structural and Refractory Materials for Fusion and Fission Technologies

CHARACTERIZATION TOOLS AND TECHNIQUES

KK: Electron Microscopy Across Hard and Soft Materials
LL: Focused Ion Beams for Analysis and Processing
MM: Magnetic Resonance in Material Science

GENERAL INTEREST

X: Frontiers of Materials Research
NN: Scientific Basis for Nuclear Waste Management XXX
OO: Actinides—Basic Science, Applications, and Technology
PP: Materials Research at High Pressure
QQ: Solid-State Chemistry of Inorganic Materials VI

MEETING ACTIVITIES

SYMPOSIUM TUTORIAL PROGRAM

Available only to meeting registrants, the symposium tutorials will concentrate on new, rapidly breaking areas of research.

EXHIBIT

A major exhibit encompassing the full spectrum of equipment, instrumentation, products, software, publications, and services is scheduled for November 28–30 in the Hynes Convention Center. Convenient to the technical session rooms and scheduled to complement the program, the MRS Fall Exhibit offers everything you need all under one roof.

PUBLICATIONS DESK

A full display of over 915 books will be available at the MRS Publications Desk.

STUDENT OPPORTUNITIES

Graduate students planning to attend the 2006 MRS Fall Meeting are encouraged to apply for a Symposium Assistant position and/or a Graduate Student Award.

CAREER CENTER

A Career Center for MRS members and meeting attendees will be open Tuesday through Thursday.

The 2006 MRS Fall Meeting will serve as a key forum for discussion of interdisciplinary leading-edge materials research from around the world.

Various meeting formats—oral, poster, round-table, forum and workshop sessions—are offered to maximize participation.

narrative threads

Narrative Threads consists of eight unique, high quality oral history interviews with key British textile artists from the mid twentieth century. All of the artists have played a significant role in the development of interdisciplinary textiles teaching, research and scholarship, predominately at Goldsmiths College, University of London, UK. Their work is nationally and internationally recognised as challenging, and changing perceptions of textiles as an art form within visual and material culture.

The box set of DVDs is an invaluable resource for students, academics and artists. It is an essential tool of reference for everyone interested and concerned with textile culture. Narrative Threads is a collaboration between Goldsmiths College and the University of the West of England, Bristol.

These DVD's are region zero (0) PAL fromat

To be launched May 2006
Priced at £160 + VAT
To order Narrative Threads please contact
the Constance Howard Resource and
Research Centre in Textiles

Constance Howard Resource
and Research Centre in Textiles

Goldsmiths College,
University of London
Deptford Town Hall (basement)
New Cross Rd,
London SE14 6AF

Tel: 020 7717 2210
e: connitex@gold.ac.uk
www.goldsmiths.ac.uk/constance-howard